DRUNK ON Confidence

UNAPOLOGETICALLY ME...
FROM LOST & ANXIOUS TO
SELF-ASSURED.

HEIDI ANDERSON

First published 2022

Big Sky Publishing Pty Ltd
PO Box 303, Newport, NSW 2106, Australia
Phone: 1300 364 611
Email: info@bigskypublishing.com.au
Web: www.bigskypublishing.com.au

Cover design and typesetting: Think Productions

Front cover image: Chelsea Bates, Fliss & Co

Chelsea Bates – Fliss & Co
Maternity and Birth photos
Shopping Centre & Shed Your Shit photos

Belle Verdiglione – Biz Coach and Photographer
Shed Your Shit & Heidi's workshop photos

Jillian McHugh Weddings
Wedding photos

A catalogue record for this book is available from the National Library of Australia

ISBN: 978-1-922765-52-9 (Paperback)
ISBN: 978-1-922765-53-6 (Ebook)

Printed and bound in Australia by Griffin Press

DRUNK ON Confidence

UNAPOLOGETICALLY ME...
FROM LOST & ANXIOUS TO
SELF-ASSURED.

A memoir

HEIDI ANDERSON

www.bigskypublishing.com.au

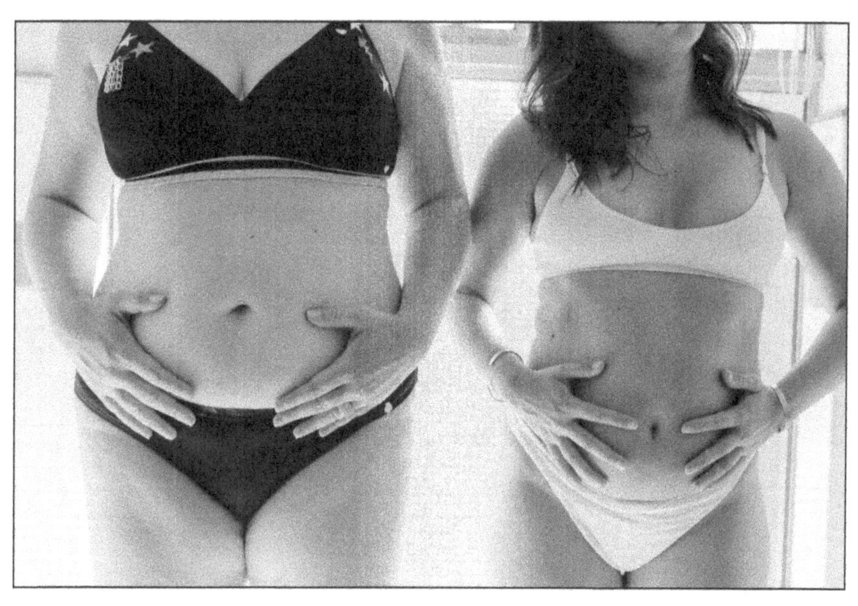

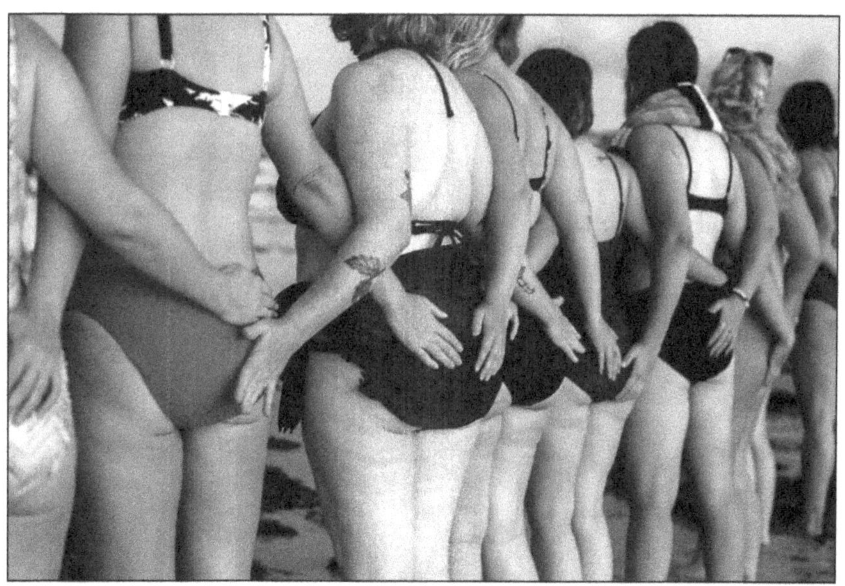

Dedication

For all the other Heidi's out there

This book is for Every BODY. Please never forget that YOU are beautiful, and you are enough just as you are.

For my family

I would like to dedicate this book to my son, Memphis, and my amazing husband, Griffo, who are my world; although I have only known you both for a very short time, you have taught me so much already. I love my boys to the moon and back.

To my dearest mum Kim, dad Steve and brother Nick, I am who I am today because of you. My family is my rock. Thank you for showing me what unconditional love is.

TESTIMONIALS

'When Heidi revealed her secret on air, it was a moment. The life of the party was disarming her demons & stepping into her power. Little did she know it would create a movement.'
– Narelda Jacobs – Channel 10 Presenter

'As someone who has struggled with confidence and body image over the years, Heidi's memoir is the kind of thing I wish I'd been given as a teenager. It would have changed my life for the better. She's not only completely inspiring in every way… she's determined to save others from suffering a similar fate. As the mother of a little girl I am so grateful there are Heidi's in the world! I'm also incredibly grateful that she manages to combine such an important story in such a compassionate, special and entertaining way!'
– Erin Molan – Sydney Breakfast Radio Host & TV Presenter

'Fate introduced me to Heidi back in 2013 when we lived together in the Big Brother house. Through the manipulated and overproduced world of reality TV we were able to forge a genuine friendship ever since. I'm so proud of the confidence Heidi has been able to create for herself and the way she now shares this with the world! In a world full of pretenders, Heidi is an inspiration on how to keep it real!'
– Tim Dormer – Big Brother Winner & TV, Radio personality

'Heidi Anderson is a straight up legend; she just gets it! She works hard, she's an ideas machine and is a content queen. Heidi is the ultimate hype girl, I know this cause she's been mine since 2013.'
– Tanya Hennessy – Comedian, TV & Radio Personality

'Heidi asked me to leave a quote about how amazing she is. That's the type of confidence she has. A brave, motivational force to be reckoned with. Constantly inspires me. Heidi has motivated me to take my top off in shopping centres also.'
– Christian Hull, Comedian – Author, Content Creator

'Heidi's perspective on life encourages me to live with more confidence every day. I will always admire her determination to help others see the positive things in life. I'M SO EXCITED FOR THIS BOOK!'
– Beck Zemek, TV personality – MAFS Contestant & Celeb Apprentice

'You will see yourself in Heidi's book. Or, you'll see your sister, daughter, wife, mum … then realise you were seeing yourself after all. Heidi Anderson is a woman who makes things happen. Not just for herself, but for the community of people she builds around her, just by being herself. Thankfully, she turned those superpowers inward to heal and this book means we all get the benefits. If you've ever succumbed to the lies of a nasty internal voice, suffered in silence, and wore a mask to get though - who hasn't? - you need Heidi's cheerleading in your life.'
– Carmen Braidwood - TV, Radio Personality & Coach

'Unique, crazy, wild souls are always drawn to each other. Sometimes you feel really alone, but people like Heidi remind us that we are connected in our own unique crazy wild ways! I always felt seen by Heidi, she is my radio soul sister. We get each other, both crazy wild spirits. Sometimes you feel lost in the world and people like Heidi make you realise that your tribe is out there. Her book will show you that you no longer have to look for answers outside of you with her incredible gift of helping you, see you.'
– Bianca Dye - TV & Radio Extraordinaire

'Real, raw and relatable! Heidi's words are the perfect combination of heart-opening and hilarious. Full of permission slips and loving reminders, *Drunk on Confidence* is the self-love bible all women need to finally stop fighting against themselves and find peace and freedom in owning and loving the skin they're in.'
– Tracey Spencer – Author, Light Worker and Biz Coach

'Heidi is the epitome of vulnerability and courage! This book is a walking permission slip for so many women to embrace their body, speak their truth and step out of their comfort zone. This memoir is refreshing and packed full of life lessons from the queen herself.'
– Rosie Rees – Founder of Naked Awakening –
Sex Toy Entrepreneur & Relationship Coach

Contents

“

BEING LOUD AND FUNNY WAS MY CRUTCH. MY CONFIDENCE FOR MOST OF MY ADULT LIFE WAS FOUND ON A SATURDAY NIGHT WHEN I WAS BINGE DRINKING.

”

INTRODUCTION

If you'd asked me a decade ago how I was so confident, I would have given you a one-word answer: champagne.

Champagne confidence: you know how you feel after a couple of glasses of bubbles? You're feeling great, self-assured and you're ready to take on the world! Well, that was me: when I was drunk, I felt confident.

After a few glasses of champagne or red wine, I was full of love for myself, I knew what I wanted and I didn't give a fuck what people thought.

I made people fall in love with my personality so that they wouldn't notice the fat girl – and it worked! People believed that I was the bubbly, funny, confident fat girl who loved to party and didn't give a shit about what people thought of me.

Being loud and funny was my crutch. My confidence for most of my adult life was found on a Saturday night when I was binge drinking.

The truth? I was masking my unhappiness with a loud, outgoing personality. I sometimes would spend hours getting ready, changing outfits 10 to 20 times in a row before heading out, and on some occasions, the anxiety wouldn't even let me make it out the front door. My close friends and family knew I had demons, as they were the ones who saw me break down. But anyone outside of my circle had no idea.

I spent years hating on myself, silencing my body demons through sex, booze and boys. The real me was invisible for most of my life, despite being the loudest person in the room. I didn't speak up because I feared judgement; I worried that people wouldn't like me anymore. I also thought that what I was going through was unique to me and no-one else would understand these thoughts, so I continued to drown out the noise.

The way I spoke to myself was disgusting, but I truly believed it. I would stand in front of the mirror hoping and praying that I would be skinny. One of my inner voices would start shouting, 'No-one will like you; you're too fat.' Then, 'How can you have any friends, looking like that? You are disgusting and fat and ugly! I hate you.' The saddest thing about this is that I truly believed these thoughts in my head, and I let them define me for years.

And then ... in 2012, during the radio show I was working on as a breakfast host, I had a life-changing breakthrough (one of many!) when I opened up on live radio about my body image and how I was genuinely feeling.

> I wish I could stand in front of you and say up yours to the guy on Facebook who told me that I had more chins than a Chinese phone book. Stuff you, to the guy who has stood before me and told me that I'd probably get a boyfriend if I lost some weight. You think that because I'm in this job that I'm confident with myself; you think that because I put myself

out there every single day, and I'm tearing up right now. I'm not as confident as what you think I am.

I wish that I could sit here and tell you that I love myself because that's what people expect me to say. But I can't – I absolutely hate my body. And every day I get up and I battle to look in the mirror. I measure myself a few times a week and I can't look in the mirror without feeling hate towards myself. I want to stop it, but I don't know how.

I've hated my body my entire life and I've battled it my entire life. Sometimes I won't leave the house because of what I see, and I'll try on 20 or so outfits because I can't decide what to wear because I hate myself when I look in the mirror. I've only just started wearing, at 28, my arms out. And its taken me this long to accept the way that I look, and everytime I look in the mirror, I really do struggle.

And every single person that I see and put myself next to, I compare myself to. At the age of 14, I struggled with an eating disorder, and I've battled my weight my whole life. Like I said, I've probably, and you'll notice this, covered up my taunts and my fears with a loud and outgoing personality. And today I stand before you telling you that I'm willing to try to love myself, to try to be happy and be in my own skin and to be the role model that people think that I am. I want to be a healthy and fit 28-year-old who doesn't beat myself up for my shape.

So today it starts right now, and it starts here. I want the strength and courage to love myself inside and out.

This moment of absolute truth on the radio changed my life forever: when I started to voice my negative, self-critical thoughts and understand why I had them … it took away their power and I began to heal.

My radio career really took off because of the rawness of this talk break, and it was shared all over Australia. I will never forget opening up *Mamamia,* one of the most read women's news pages here in Australia, to see my face all over it. And co-founder Mia Freedman, who I adored, was talking about ME on the *Mamamia Today* radio show with the hosts.

Shedding my shit that morning made me realise something else: I was not alone. In regional radio, the phone lines didn't often ring, because people were worried someone would recognise their voice, especially if they called in to talk about a personal topic like body image. But this day was different. Our lines were blocked all day by people wanting to share their stories about their body image issues. The phone lines actually didn't stop ringing after that.

With so many stories from the public being shared, we decided to put on an event for people to start the journey of loving themselves with a 'let it go' swim.

It was massive. Around a hundred people turned up to support each other and start letting go of some of the self-hate and baggage we all carried around.

A memory that I will never forget from this day, which I often replay in my mind, is when a woman in her fifties drove an hour out of her way from work just to give me a hug and say thank you. She said, 'I haven't worn shorts in 30 years, but after hearing you today, I am going out to buy myself a pair.' We both cried tears of happiness.

> "WHEN I STARTED TO VOICE MY NEGATIVE, SELF-CRITICAL THOUGHTS AND UNDERSTAND WHY I HAD THEM ... IT TOOK THEIR POWER AWAY AND I BEGAN TO HEAL."

I have shed many tears over the years and wanted to give up sometimes, but today I can stand before you and tell you that I like the way that I look.

These days you will find me rocking my red-hot bikini at the beach or standing on stages or live TV in my bra and undies preaching body positivity, self-love and acceptance. Putting myself out there can be scary by being uncomfortable, but it's how I have built my confidence.

It's been a long road to get to where I am, but it's all been worth it.

Every day I am messaged by people asking how I got to this point in my life where I have accepted who I am. What is the secret? Well, I never really doubted or disliked my personality, so this is how I got by. But I constantly struggled with my body image, and this caused debilitating anxiety for most of my twenties. It took opening up on the radio – saying my truth – to finally start to heal and make changes to get to where I am today.

For years I believed that I was the only one going through the torment I experienced because of my anxiety and poor body image. It was in those few moments on the radio when I was real, raw, honest and vulnerable that the power of those thoughts was instantly taken away. Yes, I was scared of what people were going to think and say, but the positive far outweighed the negative.

There is something hugely liberating about being honest and real about the way we feel. I know for some people this is a given, but many in our society don't want to be a burden by speaking up, so they stay quiet and battle on alone.

Being real, open, and vulnerable with the people you love is sometimes harder than telling a stranger, but I truly believe vulnerability is the first step to releasing the power of those thoughts.

It hasn't been an easy road. I remember my mate Wayne sitting me on the couch after I spoke out; he had some pretty wise words that I'll never forget. He said: 'You now need to walk the walk. Talking the talk is the easy part. You can't open up and declare that you are just going to start to love yourself without putting the work in.'

He was right. Things weren't just going to change after speaking out.

So, the hard yards began.

I started with affirmations and leaving myself love notes on the mirror. I went to hundreds of self-love workshops and read self-help book after self-help book. I gave up binge drinking – I don't need the buzz of booze to feel confident anymore.

I took up exercise and meditation.

I spoke more and more openly about the way I saw myself, trying to take away the power those inner critics had over me.

I did photo shoots in my swimwear even though I was dying inside and still a work in progress.

I wrote articles about body image, even though I was still struggling. Looking back, I think the articles were more for me than anyone else.

I'll never be perfect, but I am happy. I am so grateful for this journey I've been on, and I would like to share it with you.

I have learnt so much along the way, and I can't wait to tell you all about it.

Are you ready to be 'Drunk on Confidence'?

The Lies We Tell Ourselves and the Truth that Will Set Us Free

When I was eight years old, I never thought that my future would be blistered by self-doubt, self-hate – and the constant fear that anxiety would hold over me as an adult. I wasn't always searching for confidence through others either.

I was an extremely confident kid; I loved life and I always had a smile on my face.

My mum always said, 'You lit up every room you walked into as a kid, Heidi. Your energy and happiness always left everyone with smiles from ear to ear.'

My dad tells me the same story every time I see him: 'You smiled the day you were born, Heidi. The nurses even confirmed it wasn't wind. You really did smile. You have always been my special little girl.'

This is where Mum always jumps in: 'We were so proud, Heidi. You should've seen your dad that day; he walked the entire hospital, showing you off to everyone, yelling out, "This is my baby girl Heidi!"'

And then Heidi grew up …

“

ANNIE AND THE ANXIETY MONSTER WOULD USUALLY ARRIVE EVERY SUNDAY NIGHT AFTER A BENDER AND STAYED MOST OF THE WEEK.

ANXIOUS ANNIE AND THE ANXIETY MONSTER

It was another huge weekend in London town. We had been drinking since Friday knock-off and partied all through Saturday with no sleep – thank you, cocaine and £2 pound ecstasy tablets.

It was now Sunday night and I was lying wide awake in my bed, wondering where the fuck the weekend had gone and how I'd ended up here again.

The Anxiety Monster was on my chest, AGAIN.

And Anxious Annie, who was the ringleader of all the nasty inner voices in my head would start up. Anxious Annie is the gossip queen running around telling all the others little secrets about me. She's a true mean girl. And I know all the women out there are well acquainted with that inner mean girl. She's a real b-i-t-c-h. Top notch. Manipulative. Paranoid.

Annie's voice was loud and clear in my head:

Why did you sleep with him, Heidi? You are so disgusting.

He is never going to be your boyfriend, so stop with all the fairy tales. It was just sex for him, and he was sooooo drunk.

You will never be ... good enough, pretty enough, skinny enough.

Did you really believe that he would like you or that this time would be different?

It's because you are fat and overweight.

Maybe once you lose some weight, someone will love you.

Diet starts tomorrow.

Annie and the Anxiety Monster would usually arrive every Sunday night after a bender and stayed most of the week. The only time they weren't really there was on Friday and Saturday nights, but then again, I wasn't really there either.

Most of my weekends in London were spent partying with friends, sleeping with strangers and eating KFC on the way home after a massive Sunday session.

It was normal for us to go out Friday night, Saturday and Sunday. How we kept going was cheap pills, cocaine and pints of cider.

I was and always have been a party girl. I was known as the crazy one and was always the loudest in the room. I loved this title, because I was definitely not the skinniest or the prettiest, so I embraced being the loudest and most fun. This title fuelled my confidence, especially when I was drunk; it also fed my anxiety.

Most of the men we met in London wanted to sleep with my best mates. They never saw me as anything other than the 'funny fat friend'. Well, this is what I believed for most of my life anyway ... They always wanted to hang with me and drink ciders, but rarely were they attracted to me.

“

MY WEEKS WERE FULL OF DIETS AND ME BEATING MYSELF UP, TRYING SO HARD TO ERASE THE WEEKEND JUST GONE.

This has been my norm for most of my life, and one of the reasons why I always fall into the funny, self-deprecating role when in groups of friends and random men. I thought sleeping with men on the weekend was building my confidence because when I was hooking up with these strangers, I felt powerful, beautiful and like I had won the lottery.

My self-worth felt fierce and unstoppable when they would laugh at my jokes the next morning after a wild night of random sex.

But then they would leave, and I would be left alone in a sea of self-doubt and hate.

Sunday nights felt like a nightmare sometimes; the self-hatred and shame I experienced after the weekend was why I could never get to sleep.

My weeks were full of diets and me beating myself up, trying so hard to erase the weekend just gone.

But come Thursday, I was ready to do it all over again.

I was keen to feel that confidence again and to be loved by a stranger, even if it was just for 24 hours.

"

I'VE LIVED WITH A NUMBER OF NEGATIVE VOICES IN MY HEAD, AND THEY HAVE DRIVEN ME TO HELL AND BACK - AND I BELIEVED EVERY SINGLE THING THEY EVER TOLD ME!

MEET MY OTHER MEAN GIRL INNER CRITICS

For years I felt alone, like I was the only one feeling such self-hatred and negativity and hearing voices. I now realise that my mind isn't too dissimilar to other people's. The voices in my head might have different names, but the end game's the same. There is an 'us' not just a 'me' when it comes to how our minds work. We all have this circus going on in our minds that no-one else can hear. It can be a vicious narrative of self-doubt and anxiety combined with fear of judgement and rejection.

We all have inner critics – the mean girls in our mind. You've met Anxious Annie. She was my main critic. Then there was Negative Nelly. She was loud, obnoxious, and just would not shut up. In addition, my Nelly is negative, needy, and worst of all, she has no confidence.

Negative Nelly continually doubts herself and sees the bad before the good in every situation. I picture her to be this mini-Heidi, jumping around in my head, screaming at the top of her lungs. She is always the first to stamp her feet and is always the loudest. She's the worst kind of shock jock. These taunts and statements from Nelly were constant for a very long time:

> *You're so fat in that outfit, people will be horrified if you wear that tonight. Take it off, you're a fatty.*
>
> *Oh, I can't believe you said that; people must think you're so dumb.*
>
> *As if that guy will stick around; he'll eventually leave you. You're so not good enough for him.*

You could be thinking that I'm super crazy, but more than likely a lightbulb has just gone off and you're thinking, 'Shit, I have one of those too.'

Guess what? I have more than one voice and you'll meet all of them in this book.

Most of us are told some form of bullshit by the voices in our heads:

> *I will be worth loving when I'm more attractive.*
>
> *I will be worth loving when others love me.*
>
> *I will love myself when I am more successful.*
>
> *I will love myself when I feel worthy.*

They are really saying the same thing: *I am not worth loving.*

Lucky for me, and you, these are lies. And I'll give you the truth: You are worthy of love.

Throughout my life I've lived with a number of negative voices in my head, and they have driven me to hell and back – and I believed every single thing they ever told me!

Nelly is my negative BFF. Then there's Nelly's little sister Sally. Nelly was always negative about everything, not just me and my body. But Self-loathing Sally wasn't quite as well-rounded. She was laser focused on my tummy flab, the slight lump in the top or pants and the zit on my forehead. Sally hated everything about my body, and I have no idea why. It was just always her default to hate me. Pick on me. Harass me.

I want you to meet Polly too. I feel like People-pleasing Polly is in all of us. She does what everyone else wants to do. She has no original thoughts or ideas. She does whatever the other three want, unless someone who isn't a disembodied voice in my head wants something else. And then she tells me I have to do that. She always takes a dare. But it didn't matter how much I tried to please Anxious Annie, or my other inner critics, they never shut up. It only made them more insistent. One more drink. One more puff. One more guy.

Finally, there is Comparison Cassie, who pretty much knocks around with all of them. Cassie has been around most of my life too, but she got really loud during my high school years when all the boys I liked seemed to like my friends. Nowadays, many of us have to listen to Cassie when we're scrolling social media. She might even turn up when you're reading this book.

In this book, I'll show you how you can make friends with all these mean gals.

Once I owned my shit (you'll find out what this means later) I understood who these voices were and why they had taken up residence in my mind. The biggest realisation I had was that I didn't have to believe what these mean gals were telling me. For years, they ruled my life, and I took every word they said as gospel. Gaining an awareness around these voices and what they had me believing had a huge impact because I could finally see the lies for what they were. LIES!

I now have a new toolkit filled with tips and tools to stop lies like 'I am not good enough' from being a core belief.

It wasn't easy. There is no magic pill to erase anxiety. Even if you choose to medicate, you still need to be aware of your triggers so that you can manage the daily noise those mean gals can throw your way. I tell you this so that when your own Annie, Nelly or Sally starts telling you that this won't happen because you're a failure or – insert whatever your voice is telling you – you can combat this by saying, 'Heidi told me this was hard, but she also said I'm worth it.'

You're worth it!

The first step for me was getting real with these voices in my head and questioning the stories they were telling me. 'You can't do that. You're not pretty enough to be successful. You're not worthy. You suck. You will never be like them ...' I knew I was having these thoughts, but I didn't know that it was okay for me to not believe them. I just assumed they were right and that something was wrong with me, because no-one else seemed to be having this daily internal battle with their own mind; I assumed that everyone else was fine!

I got brutally honest with myself about how I was playing the victim, judging others and myself, comparing, controlling, and people-pleasing to be liked – I started to take responsibility for my own life.

I was the only one who could make the changes in my life to stop drinking so much and sleeping around.

I was responsible for loving and accepting myself. No-one else!

I was in charge of my life, but I was giving away my power to strangers daily.

The reality is that you can't make positive changes in your life until you're honest about the things that aren't making you feel good anymore. This includes the negative thoughts you keep having.

“

THE BEST THING I EVER DID FOR MY ANXIETY WAS TELLING PEOPLE ABOUT WHAT WAS HAPPENING – REALLY SHEDDING MY SHIT.

SPEAKING MY TRUTH

My girlfriend asked me once how my anxious brain works. I told her it's like jumping on a merry-go-round every day, and you just go round and round and round and round. And you can't get off. The merry-go-rounds I went on as a kid were fun, but you could hop off. This one will send you into a spiral of insanity and self-destruction, spinning faster and faster with irrational thoughts, and fears building and overtaking your brain.

You wholeheartedly believe the stories you're telling yourself, no-one can convince you otherwise. They can try, but once you're in that deep, dark place it can be very hard to get out of it. So, when you hop off that merry-go-round you're layered up with all the lies – the shit that you let stick – and then the next day you queue up and get on … again!

I have been very lucky. After I shared my story publicly, let my guard down and finally spoke out about how fat, loud, successful Heidi wasn't really dealing with life – that I was in fact broken – the support and love I have been shown from around the globe has filled my heart. There are so many versions of how we hurt ourselves. But all we need to do is ask for help. Unfortunately, some people still feel are alone. If this is you, then my story is for you. Let's tackle 'this' together.

I solemnly swear that the best thing I ever did for my anxiety was telling people about what was happening – really shedding my shit – taking off the layers that Sally, Nelly, Annie, Cassie and Polly had helped build, blocking the 'real' Heidi. Just sharing my story helped me out of the darkness. When I spoke about my anxiety on the radio, I was inundated with messages of support and love, and people wanting to share their own stories from all around the world. People stopped me on the street to speak to me about their anxiety. I had been suffering for a very long time, but I never really understood what was going on. So, I drowned the anxious feeling *every* weekend with copious amounts of red wine, ciggies and recreational drugs.

Sometimes I would come across as disconnected, not all there, moody, agitated, aggressive and stressed, and people often wondered what they had done wrong. But they'd done nothing wrong! My anxiety had taken over my entire body and I was full of fear. It could and would happen in any situation, especially if I was pushed out of my comfort zone, or if I thought I was losing control. Colleagues, friends and family often saw it and just thought, 'Oh, that's Heidi', and the most exhausting part was that in every situation like this, I would spend days, sometimes even weeks, beating myself up for the way I reacted.

Today, it's a different story. Now, everyone knows I experience anxiety, so they can better understand my behaviour and can empathise and not take things personally. This kind of fear doesn't just disappear, and it will never fully go away, but I have learnt to embrace it, and I now understand it a whole lot better.

I had a wealth of support from listeners who had heard my story, who helped me understand that I wasn't alone, and also in a way made me accountable for what I did next, but I understand that this isn't going to be the stepping stone for everyone (hell, I didn't think it would be mine). I do know that the support of just one person who is constantly in your corner is the true gold. Your next step might be texting a friend, or booking an appointment with your local doctor to talk about your mental health, or even finding a coach to be your support as you start to own your shit. I know it can be scary as fuck speaking out, especially when your Anxious Annie pipes up to tell you, 'No-one has time for your crap! Why would they listen to you? Stop feeling sorry for yourself and get on with it.'

I get it; I was you too.

But I know now the power of being vulnerable and I want you to know that you are not alone.

I see you.

Conquering Self-Loathing with Self-Love

Self-Loathing Lie #1

I'll love myself when I'm more attractive

♥

Self-Loving Truth #1

My body deserves love just the way it is!
I will feed it and exercise it because I love it

“

EVERY TIME I LOOKED IN THE MIRROR, I WOULD HEAR SELF-LOATHING SALLY. FROM THEN ON, MY WEIGHT BEGAN TO INCREASE.

SELF-LOATHING SALLY

So many of us say, 'I'll love myself when …'

Well, when is *now*. I wasted years feeding myself bullshit lies like:

I am not good enough.

I am fat.

I am not the 'perfect' weight.

I am not pretty enough.

I am ugly.

I am not worthy of love.

I'll be successful when I am skinny.

If any of this sounds familiar, then you have met your Self-loathing Sally. She spent a shitload of my life bringing me down and constantly taunting me about my weight and making me feel like I was not good enough. Sally started rearing her ugly little head quite early in my life. I remember the first time I met her, I was around seven years old and some boys in primary school had been calling me names. 'Miss Piggy' was one that really stuck. As the name-calling continued, Sally got really loud and she would chirp in whenever I was getting dressed, saying things like, 'Your tummy doesn't look good in that.' 'Are you sure you want to wear that?' 'Everyone thinks you're fat. You are fat; look at you, Miss Piggy.'

As much as I tried to ignore Sally, her opinions were constantly validated by other people and boy oh boy did Sally love that; she just got louder and louder. I still remember her sarcastic comment when I was in high school and the boy, I was dating dumped me after our very first date. In his 'breakup letter' he didn't mention my weight as being part of his decision, but his mates were not so polite, saying that he thought I was too fat to go out with.

I can still hear Sally's response to this day: 'I told you so!' And I believed her.

Sally was always there to deliver the self-loathing punch, and, I simply didn't have anything in my own self-help tool kit to say 'Well, screw them, I'm good enough' or even 'What would they know?!'

“

I CONSTANTLY COMPARED MYSELF TO OTHERS. I LET THE OPINIONS OF OTHERS RULE MY LIFE. IT TOOK 35 YEARS OF MY LIFE TO TAKE THAT POWER BACK.

EATING MY FEELINGS

I grew up in a country town, Bathurst, in Australia, with your typical middle-class family. Never, ever did anyone in my family tell me I was fat. Okay, that's a lie; I think my brother did when we had fights, but he is forgiven now. My parents always showed me love and are two of the kindest people you will ever meet.

Mum just recently sold her coffee shop in Bathurst, which she ran for 32 years. I have never met harder working parents. Growing up, I never really noticed my mum's issue with her weight or the fact that she is an emotional eater also. I say also because it was only in the past few years when I was on my path of self-development that I had an *aha* moment: I was too.

I ate when I was happy.

I ate when I was sad.

I ate when I was nervous.

I ate when I was anxious.

I ate when I was stressed.

Not only did I realise that I'd been eating my feelings away forever, I realised Mum and Nan had both been doing the exact same thing. Monkey see, monkey do. And let me be clear that I do not believe for a moment that my own battle with weight, self-worth and anxiety is anything other than my own. My bullshit lies were developed over decades.

Mum never made me feel less than – if anything – she did her best to teach me how to love myself and not give a fuck what anyone else thought of me. She always made it clear that the opinions of others didn't matter. If you are happy with the way you saw yourself, then why listen to anyone else? But in my teens, it wasn't cool to listen to my mum, so I always did the opposite. Instead of running my own race and listening to my wise mum, I followed the crowd. I became self-obsessed and I constantly compared myself to others. I let the opinions of others rule my life. It took 35 years of my life to take that power back.

My family, my mum, my dad had my back – Sally, on the other hand, didn't have my best interests at heart. I still remember my first kiss like it was yesterday. I was so fucking nervous. It was with a boy called Matty; everyone was egging us on to pash in front of them at the park, so we did. I felt chuffed with myself that I had just kissed a bloke like they do in the movies, French style.

Sally wasn't anywhere to be seen or heard. I was flying high on the kiss when I heard one of Matty's friends whisper to him, 'You kissed the fat girl.' My heart sank, and within minutes, Sally was there with her marching band screaming at the top of her lungs, 'Told you it was too good to be true. You're fat. See it was a joke. He will never like you. You're too fat!"

After my first kiss, Sally pretty much took up residence, and she was never really far from any kind of happy thoughts.

Every time I looked in the mirror, I would hear Self-loathing Sally. From then on, my weight began to increase.

But still, my mum and my dad would never comment on my weight. Dad has always been my biggest cheerleader; even when I hit my heaviest, he never once said I was fat.

Dad has had his business for almost 40 years. I am so similar to him. We both wear our hearts on our sleeve and are go-getters at whatever we put our minds to. Growing up, I was always Daddy's little girl.

It was in Year 9 when I was at an all-girls high school that everyone started to really care and worry about what everyone else looked like. The judgement was fierce, and the pressure was next level. My weight had ballooned, even after my doctor told me that I was obese and needed to lose some weight. Not once did my parents comment, but Mum did suggest Weight Watchers because that's what had worked for her in her teens and she thought it would help teach me how to make healthy life-long choices.

This backfired. I became obsessed. My relationship with food became negative. I started using words like 'good and bad' when I spoke about foods. My fascination with how much weight I lost or gained became an obsession. I have only just broken this obsession in the past few years. I spiralled and soon developed disordered eating. I can still see myself on the phone to my best friend at the time, crying that I had put on 200 grams at my weigh-in. I now know that this could've been a poo, that 200 grams is nothing. I was also competing with another girl in my year who was at Weight Watchers too. This is when Comparison Cassie was born. I was constantly worried about how much weight she'd lost and if she looked skinnier in clothes than I did.

I have since been on every diet ever created and yo-yoed more than Oprah Winfrey and I am half her age. The most fucked-up thing about this situation, which kept Self-loathing Sally well and truly alive, was that when I hit my thinnest, I had the boys at school wanting to hook up with me and date me. I had the hottest and coolest guy ask me out to a debutant ball; he wouldn't have even known my name when I was fat.

I said yes and we hung out a few times, but this created a monster in me, and the bullshit lie I told myself for years afterwards – 'I'll be successful when I am skinny' – was etched in my unconscious brain from here onwards.

“

I SPENT YEARS SEARCHING FOR LOVE AND AFFIRMATION THROUGH ONE-NIGHT STANDS, BOOZE AND DRUGS.

CHASING HAPPINESS – BOYS, BOOZE AND BAD DECISIONS

I'll never forget when I drank myself silly at a party, sculling every alcoholic beverage in sight, all because a boy had kissed my friend. This time it felt different though, it hurt so much deeper than before ... because I'd been kissing the same boy only a week prior and we'd been talking on the phone every day. He was supposed to be at the party for me. I spent the rest of the night vomiting in the toilets while she kissed him on the dance floor. You can imagine what Sally was saying after that.

A few years later, I met my high school sweetheart, Patty. We then spent the next six years breaking up and getting back together. It was young love for us, and we were both incredibly immature. I thought I couldn't live without him and was super needy. He was battling his own demons. He was my first love and one I will never forget. Although we fought every time we went out drinking together, never did he ever bring up my weight. He loved me through every size I was in our six years.

After we broke up, I spent years searching for love and affirmation through one-night stands, booze and drugs. I was living in London with a bunch of girlfriends after Patty and I broke up and if we weren't drunk, we were high. I still longed to feel worthy of love. My heart was broken, and I no longer loved Patty, but Sally had me believing that no-one would ever love me again. I was desperate for some kind of validation, and I searched for it on every night out, almost always ending up with some random guy. Sally was really quiet on these nights out. I was wiping her out with every shot I'd knock back or every line of cocaine I'd snort. But by the morning, she would be back with her gang members, Anxious Annie and Negative Nelly, louder than the day before.

I was in Europe with my best friends working and partying at Oktoberfest. I was having a great time with my girlfriends but behind the wild, loud, confident fat girl, I was longing to be loved. My friends were all thin and very beautiful and every guy I ever liked 'just wanted to be friends' but was keen to hook up with my very good-looking friend. This was something I had seen my whole life; so, time and time again Sally's comments were being verified by the men I surrounded myself with.

I finally met someone at Beerfest in Germany. We got along like a house on fire and he treated me like a queen. We were always laughing and pulling the piss out of each other. He never, ever mentioned my weight and I felt like it wasn't an issue. Every time we hung out it was always the same. When we all moved back to London, we would hang out and get drunk, sometimes sleeping together but not always. It was nice to feel like I was moving on from Patty and that someone else was showing me the attention I craved so badly.

We were at a party one night and I had his phone in my bag. I was out the front having a ciggie when a text came through, and I couldn't stop myself … I had to read it. My heart sank. The text message he received wasn't bad. It was what he'd sent.

There on the screen was what Sally had been looking for all along. The message read: 'Hey, man, yeah, we did it again this morning. Me and the fat one. See you tonight.'

We'd slept together that morning, and hung out all day, so it couldn't be anyone else. Sally started spiralling and next minute I was leaving the party with his phone, just so I could read that message over and over again.

Read text: 'Me and the fat one.'

Read text again: 'Me and the fat one.'

This kept playing over and over like a broken record. Tears ran down my face as I ran through the dark streets of London. Sally was yelling by this stage, 'Again! Wake up! He was always going to see you for the fat fuck that you are. Of course, he didn't like you. Did you really think he would want to be with a fat fuck?'

The sad thing is, I ran to his house and waited for him and the others to return. I felt so low at that stage but was desperate to be loved and feel worthy that I waited for him to come home and then pretended that nothing was wrong. My best friend couldn't hold back. It was all put on the table, but somehow it got turned around on us and we were the evil ones for reading his text messages. Sally loved to read text messages like this, and so did all her gang members. They weren't going anywhere.

Sally, Nelly, Annie, Cassie and Polly exist in most of us. Many women have shared with me their similar stories and bullshit lies they tell themselves. We are born with the confidence to be ourselves and love ourselves but society's pressures and influence takes their toll, and we convince ourselves that we are not good enough.

“

YOU HAVE TO START TO BELIEVE IT: SOCIAL MEDIA ISN’T REAL. SO, STOP COMPARING YOURSELF TO EVERYONE ON THERE.

BUYING INTO THE MEDIA'S NARRATIVE

I love social media and have worked really hard at my relationship with it, but I can totally understand the negativity most of us have towards it, because I have been there.

The comments on Facebook pages, the trolling, the constant comparisons, and because I was in the public eye, I was free game. My job choices played to my strengths – that funny, entertaining, try hard and harder Heidi. But it also offered up what was left to be sacrificed to the 'faceless' social media trolls.

In the end, I stopped reading comments on my work social media and just focused on my pages. But it's not just trolls or horrible comments that makes social media toxic at times; it's who we follow. Realising this was a big moment in my self-development journey.

Comparison Cassie loves to bring you down when you're on social media, which we've all been brainwashed to believe is the 'real world'. How we view women on this platform controls the way we act and feel. I know you would've heard it a million times already but for fuck's sake, you have to start to believe it: social media isn't real. So, STOP comparing yourself to everyone on there. Filters are fake and 99 per cent of people are only posting highlights of their life. Just because you spend most of your time checking the app doesn't mean you're seeing their entire lives. It's snippets, so STOP with the judgement. This one really frustrates me. These posts and pictures are produced in the same way as reality TV shows. It's not real!

TV shows, magazines, books, industries and adverts are all to blame for the way we see ourselves and the bullshit lies we then believe. The way they use marketing to brainwash you into thinking that your tiger stripes aren't beautiful or that the cellulite you have on your thighs needs to be fixed is why we all don't feel worthy or good enough at times.

Growing up, I couldn't relate to anyone in magazines or on TV shows. There was no celebrity in the 1980s and 90s that I can remember being celebrated for her bigger frame. My mum used to buy the trashy mags every Monday and I used to steal them to look at all the photos and check out their diet tips that were plastered all over the front covers. The only time I ever saw someone in these mags, who resembled my size, they were being told to lose weight. This narrative of women not being thin enough if they were your standard size 14 was controlled by the media. And I bought into the narrative as a vulnerable teenager. I believed what they were selling me and took it as gospel: 'Being skinny means you are successful.' This lie stayed with me for almost 20 years.

I remember watching the very first season of *Australian Idol*, in 2003, when Ian 'Dicko' Dickson famously told one of the singers, Paulini Curuenavuli, on national TV she should 'choose more appropriate clothes or shed some pounds'. Paulini was 21 at the time and she had just belted out an incredible version of Destiny's Child's 'Survivor'; her voice was not even mentioned but her weight was. At 20 years of age myself, seeing this just played into my belief that being skinny means you are successful.

I have been many sizes, and for most of my teens and twenties I was defined by the number on the tag and the number on the scales.

LIFE IS TOO SHORT TO CRY OVER A NUMBER ON THE SCALES.

DITCH THE SCALES

One of the big pieces of life-changing advice I can give you, which I wish someone had told me earlier on in life, was so simple: 'Stop weighing yourself!' If you know that every time you jump on the scales your mood changes, you eat and drink more because you are emotional, or you become even more obsessed, then you have to stop. Life is too short to cry over a number on the scales and believe me, I have done that plenty of times.

I stopped weighing myself over six years ago. It took me a while, but I have finally given up the scales! Weighing myself is a major trigger that I'd prefer to live without these days. I don't know how much I weigh and that makes me really happy. When I need to be weighed for some reason, I ask them kindly to not let me know what the number is because I have wasted too much of my life worried and obsessed by it. When I was pregnant and had to be weighed at every doctor's appointment, I asked them to not announce my weight. They understood this was a trigger, and to this day I have no idea how much weight I put on while I was pregnant or how much I have lost or gained since.

I can almost guarantee that one of the reasons my anxiety has disappeared around my body image is because I have stopped chasing a number. I stopped joining weight loss challenges and I started to eat and train for my health and wellbeing, not because I feared I'd become fat or overweight.

For years I've signed up for these challenges and it never made me happy. I developed this habit when I started Weight Watchers as a teenager, and it has only been in the last few years that I have been able to kick the torture after living most of my life like this.

I still remember, clear as day, getting weighed in at Weight Watchers. I can still see all the women in the room, waiting patiently with their progress books. No-one ever really talked; you could feel the shame in the air, emanating from every person.

I would hop on the scales. I wouldn't make eye contact with the lady just in case the scales tipped the wrong way. If they did and I didn't lose weight, my entire week was ruined.

I had failed.

I was not worthy, and it was the end of the world.

This turned into disordered eating for me for years and years.

The cycle of self-loathing and shame was my norm, right up until I was in my thirties.

It's been a long road to recovery, but I am finally free from the emotional and mental torture I experienced around food, scales and exercise. I conquered self-loathing with self-love.

These days, I live by the following mantras:

I exercise or train to keep healthy and fit.

I eat joyfully to fuel my body.

Exercise for your mental health, not for your waistline.

“

I'M STILL A WORK IN PROGRESS, BUT I CAN HAPPILY TELL YOU THAT THIS OBSESSION WITH MY WEIGHT DOES NOT RULE MY LIFE ANYMORE.

Food and my weight are on my mind less and less.

The guilt and shame I have around the food I consume is becoming obsolete.

And since I stopped weighing myself I have noticed I'm also less aware of what size I'm wearing. Numbers used to define my day and mood whether they were on the scales or my pants.

I'm still a work in progress, but I can happily tell you that this obsession with my weight does not rule my life anymore.

I'm finally free from the scales.

Let me tell you a little story: when I trained with a group at my local gym a few years ago, a lady in the group asked me why I didn't weigh in. At first I felt embarrassed, but then I explained to her that I'd quit the scales a couple of years ago. She responded with a big smile and said, 'That's great that you can do that.' I walked away proud with a big grin on my face thinking, 'Hell yeah, I've got this.'

I don't have to be like everyone else. I have to do what works for me and what makes me happy. Yes, I still want to be healthy, but I go by how my clothes feel and fit now, not by the number on the scale or the label.

YOU HAVE THE CHOICE TO CHANGE THE STORY ABOUT YOURSELF AND THE WAY YOU EXERCISE AND TAKE CARE OF YOURSELF.

WORK OUT TO FEEL GOOD, NOT FOR WEIGHT LOSS

One of the mottos I live by now is this: exercise for your mental health, not for your waistline.

When you start to like yourself, you start to look after yourself. I really noticed this in my late twenties when I moved to Bunbury, Western Australia for my radio career. For the majority of my twenties, I exercised on and off, but I only ever worked out with one goal in mind and that was to lose weight. I didn't go to the gym or for walks because it felt good and made my endorphins run wild throughout my body; no, I worked out because I knew that it would help me lose weight.

It was *always* a punishment.

When I first moved to Bunbury, I was introduced to a guy called Pete Stokes who owned the local boxing gym. He said he would train me three times a week and that he did. I am not sure I loved the exercise as much as his company because if you could ask him, he'd tell you I abused him every session until I started to see results. Sadly, Pete passed away in 2018 after battling cancer. He was a true inspiration for me; he is the reason I fell in love with training and working out. Pete and his partner Jodie taught me to care for myself and I have been training ever since.

I no longer work out because I want to lose weight. I now train four times a week because it makes me feel good and I like myself. I am a huge advocate for exercising for your mental health. I have noticed a massive change in my mental state since I shifted my thinking around working out and why I do it. Anxious Annie would turn up and start beating me up and put pressure on me to work out five to six times a week. But I realised that when I put that pressure on myself, I gave myself unwarranted anxiety.

It took time and patience to make these changes but removing goals from my workout routine was the key to success for me. I also stopped weighing myself and writing down calories. For far too long I was defined by numbers, so training myself to let that go, took time and patience but making these changes decreased my anxiety and increased my happiness.

I would also suggest that you only do exercise that you enjoy. If you dislike group fitness classes, then stop. Find what works for you then do it a few times a week. I find walking and running really boring, so I change it up on the treadmill and do a minute of running and a minute of walking and it works for me. I also try to walk with friends or at the beach instead of having coffee dates. Or I find a really great podcast and I walk for the length of that. My brain doesn't like big numbers either, so I choose to do circuit training instead of hour-long sweat sessions. If I see 60 minutes on the clock, my negative way of thinking will take over and I don't enjoy the session at all. So small one-to-five–minute rounds of exercises work best for me.

“

I NOW TRAIN FOUR TIMES A WEEK BECAUSE IT MAKES ME FEEL GOOD AND I LIKE MYSELF.

I'm often asked how I fit my training in around my ever-changing schedule and the answer is simple: I make it a priority! When I was working in breakfast radio, if I didn't go to the gym straight after work, the excuses would start. If I didn't go to the gym and came home to eat first, I made a promise to myself that I needed to get a workout in before I hit a wall at 3pm. This is when I discovered workouts on YouTube. This was a life saver for me! There is every single kind of workout you can think of online and at your fingertips to suit every level of fitness. I love setting up my laptop in the backyard and smashing out a half-hour workout; it really is that simple and there is no excuse. Some workouts I love online are Body Fit by Amy and Yoga with Adriene.

Let your mental health motivate you to work out!

You have the choice to change the story about YOURSELF and the way you exercise and take care of yourself. Instead of thinking negatively about parts of yourself, you can start celebrating you and embracing all parts of you.

You do not need permission from anyone to change. You have the power to choose how you want to talk about yourself, stop handing it over to everyone else. If you're covered in those beautiful tiger stripes FUCK it, they are yours to keep forever, and I hear patterns are in! If you still have curves and excess weight, remember that it's more for your lover to hold on to! Rock your curves and embrace them. Tomorrow isn't guaranteed.

If your mum pouch is still there months, weeks or years later ... who gives a flying fuck? I actually don't want mine to disappear because it's a constant reminder of what my body did.

Don't ever be ashamed of cellulite. Dimples are cute whether they're on your butt cheeks or face cheeks. So, stop covering up!

My body and your body deserve to be loved just the way they are. Stop buying into the media's narrative, listening to your inner critics, or worrying about other people think. You are enough just as you are.

Conquering People-Pleasing with Self-Kindness

Self-Loathing Lie #2

I'll love myself when others love me

♥

Self-Loving Truth #2

Others can show you the way to loving yourself, but ultimately, it's up to you

UNDERNEATH THAT SMILE AND FAKE CONFIDENCE WAS A YOUNG INSECURE GIRL DESPERATE FOR VALIDATION AND FOR PEOPLE TO LOVE HER.

PEOPLE-PLEASING POLLY

I think because I felt as though everyone else loved me, that was enough. Being the funny fat girl, I was always going out of my way to please others and make them laugh, putting their needs before mine. People-pleasing Polly showed her face in high school. She was around occasionally in the earlier years, but she decided to join me for good in my teens.

The silly thing was that my parents always showed me love and attention so I cannot blame them for the way I felt. I probably only realised that I was a people pleaser when I met Griffo, my now husband. He is my knight in shining armour. He taught me how to love myself when I thought loving myself was impossible. He has taught me through his actions towards himself and through the way that he sees me. They say you can't fall in love unless you love yourself first, but I call bullshit on that because I didn't have a whole lot of love for myself when we met, and he still fell in love with me. It took me a while to get to where I am, but he has by far been my greatest teacher. To him, I have always just been Heidi, his 'sexy girl'.

Griffo helped me find and build the confidence I lacked. He taught me that beauty is what's on the inside, and he showed me how to let go of many of my hang-ups. It was around the time that Griffo and I started dating that I decided to invest in self-development and go on the journey of self-love, so he has seen all of me. We met five years before we started dating, when we were both living in London, so he has seen the crazy, loud, boisterous Heidi also. Five years later we reunited at one of our best friend's birthdays, and we have been together ever since.

I was in my third year of breakfast radio, living in Newcastle, and he was in Perth, so we did the whole long-distance thing until I was moved to Perth for work after *Big Brother*. I know! You didn't see that coming, did you? Well, in 2013, I entered the *Big Brother* house and was booted out on day 43. This was not good for People-pleasing Polly's ego. Looking back now, it's probably one of the reasons I was voted out; I was trying too hard to please everyone else. I wasn't being honest about how I was truly feeling because I didn't want people to hate me.

Working in breakfast radio for almost 10 years and going on *Big Brother* really weren't great for Polly. I don't have any regrets because I am who I am today because of these experiences, but what I have realised now is that both of these things really fed into my ego and Polly's. Every day I was desperate for people to like me. I was searching for validation daily from people for a laugh. The funny fat girl who was desperate to please others found her calling in radio in 2010 as an outgoing funny girl, but underneath that smile and fake confidence was a young insecure girl desperate for validation and for people to love her. I fed myself to the lions, but I am so fucking thankful I have done this because I know now that I am one resilient motherfucker.

“

I WAS CONSTANTLY TRYING TO PLEASE SOMEONE, AND THAT SHIT GETS TIRING.

I still remember the first negative comment I received online when I was working in Bunbury: a guy told me I was 'fat and not funny at all and to get off his radio'. It cut me to my core. I can still feel my heart sink and my tummy flip. I can still hear People-pleasing Polly in my head: 'Why wouldn't this guy think I was funny? What did I say? How can I make him like me?' And around and around I would go on the merry-go-round. I would often respond to these comments by trying to make them laugh so they would like me. Sometimes it worked. I then spent the next 10 years trying to get people to like me on the radio.

When I sit back and reflect on what I know now, I think about how bad at times being in the public eye was for my self-esteem. After almost every radio show in my regional radio days, we would have a post-show debrief which pretty much meant you would be told by a boss or a co-worker what you did wrong on that show and how you could do it better. Some days they would talk about your laugh or your sense of humour. Some days they would tell you that you sucked. It's true, sometimes we did suck! They would pick apart everything you said in one talk break. That was tough, especially when I was just starting out. You really did have to have a thick skin and that is something that took me a very long time to grow.

This environment of constantly overthinking what I had done, what I should have done, fuelled my anxiety on a daily basis. And then I took on *Big Brother* – in hindsight, that really should have set some large alarm bells ringing! I was constantly trying to please someone, and that shit gets tiring. When I was in the *Big Brother* house most of the time, I felt inauthentic and unhappy because I was always on the merry-go-round in my own head questioning what I'd said or done. I was the same working in radio; I was always worried if I'd offended someone, said the wrong thing, laughed at the wrong joke, or made my boss or my co-hosts unhappy.

It was exhausting.

And, in 2016, my next on-air confession of being broken and hating myself honestly could have been the absolute worst decision I made.

I had a breakdown, or as I like to call it now, a *breakthrough.*

I call it a breakthrough thanks to Brené Brown and her deep insight from her research (if you don't know who Brené Brown is, Google her TED talk on the power of vulnerability).

“

WEARING A MASK IS EXHAUSTING AND AT SOME STAGE THE LIES WILL CATCH UP WITH YOU.

MY SECOND ON-AIR CONFESSION

In 2016, a few years into my dream job at a Perth radio station, I hit rock bottom. I was supposed to be having the time of my life, I was getting paid big bucks to do what I loved, I had the guy of my dreams and I was living like a queen.

But I wasn't …

Most days after the radio show, I went home and slept.

I was having panic attacks in the middle of the ad breaks and then running back to the microphone with a fake smile and tears running down my face.

For six weeks I'd suffered severely from anxiety, and it had affected every aspect of my life, including my job and relationship. I was asked by my boss, now friend Amanda, to describe to her what happened when I was suffering, as she wanted to understand anxiety. I went on to explain to her that every sufferer feels something different and that we will all experience a range of different symptoms and effects. Many people don't get anxiety, and often they don't recognise anxiety or mental health challenges as real illnesses. They think it's pretend because you can't see it, or not as important to address like a health issue.

In 2022, Beyond Blue stated that, '17.9% of females aged 16 to 85 experienced an anxiety disorder in the last 12 months ... In fact 1 in 3 women will experience anxiety during their lifetime.' It's the most common mental condition, can you believe that? Crazy. I believe that these statistics could be higher, with many more who suffer in silence, too afraid to speak out.

I'd been diagnosed with anxiety in 2009 after I returned from living in the UK. I now know I'd been suffering anxiety for many years before, but I never really understood what was wrong and lived with the horrible effects of it. When I recognised that I was out of control – booze, men, drugs, self-hate, the whole mess – I had 10 appointments with a psychologist. And as a result, declared myself CURED, patted myself on the back for being so in control of my future and then continued with all the same problems, gradually getting more out of control. Wearing a mask is exhausting and at some stage the lies will catch up with you.

So, when I was struggling to get out of bed and go to work, I realised that I needed to do something about my mental health, for good. I couldn't hide anymore and with the support of my friend and boss Amanda, and my co-hosts, I wrote out my darkest thoughts and feelings and read it aloud on the radio. I had shared my vulnerabilities and shed my shit on the radio before, in Bunbury 2012, when I opened up about hating myself, but this time was different. I felt like someone had taken over me and my body, I felt like a stranger to myself.

And if I was noticing it, then listeners were too. I needed to get this off my chest. The shame I was feeling, pretending to be okay, tore me up inside and I think this was what was keeping me so stuck.

I began:

> Looking back, the past few weeks are very blurry, and I've spent most of it in my head. A lot of changes have happened around me this year and that has really sent me into a downward spiral.
>
> I have been dragging my butt out of bed to get to work and then as soon as the show and work commitments are over, I'd go straight home. My partner, Griffo, has been an amazing support, considering he wouldn't know who he was getting each day.
>
> We were both on a rollercoaster depending on my level of anxiety for the day. Some days, and truthfully not many, I would come home with a smile on my face and every other day I would be sad, angry or just withdrawn.
>
> I drank alcohol almost every night. Numbing the anxiety is what made me feel alive, but then I would wake the next morning and feel 10 times worse. It's a vicious cycle and I've struggled to break free. I stopped working out and I ate almost everything in sight. I lost control. My brain has been congested with self-doubt and extremely irrational with erratic negative thoughts. I could only see the worst in situations.
>
> I find it hard to talk when I'm in the middle of an episode, which can be extremely difficult when that is my paid job. I've had panic attacks in the middle of the show and had to run to the toilets.

> I overthink almost everything. I wake in the middle of the night replaying conversations over and over in my head, Did I offend so and so when I said that? What if she hates me? I'll sometimes lay awake for hours at a time, analysing and deconstructing situations or conversations.
>
> My tummy will be full of knots and I get the runs. (Sorry, not sorry … it's the truth.) My mouth will become rigid and my cheek will tremble. My levels of paranoia skyrocket through the roof and I completely withdraw. Yet my body somehow goes into autopilot and I'm able to perform, drive, walk, work and have sex. I can't tell you what happened over the last few weeks as I have no recollection and that's scary. My mind will race to the point of exhaustion.
>
> I come to the wrong conclusions about things, and I suffer in silence as my paranoia is at extreme heights.
>
> I'm petrified of dying and this plays a huge part in my everyday – I will sometimes think about being killed or dying in a horrific car accident more than 20 times a day.
>
> Anxiety affects my life, along with so many Australians, so if you need to talk to someone about it send me a message because you are not alone.

After I shed my shit on the radio that day, I instantly felt freer. The shame I had been carrying around had disappeared. The response blew me away: I was inundated with messages on my Facebook page that took me months to respond to. The video that my radio station shared of me opening up went viral around the world.

I replied to more than a thousand messages, not just from sufferers but from family members and friends who now felt like they understood their loved one.

It was another monumental moment of vulnerability that changed my life because again I no longer felt alone and I began taking the next steps in my journey of self-love.

I also felt an incredible sense of freedom after I shed my shit, like I wasn't living a lie anymore. I actually felt lighter!

People were finally seeing the real me.

“

I DON'T NEED YOU TO REACT TOO OR GIVE ME TOUGH LOVE, I JUST NEED YOU TO HOLD ME.

FINDING MY LOVE WITH MY LOVE

Our love story didn't start off like a fairy tale, but it does end up that way.

My Prince Charming, Griffo, is one of my inspirations and had an enormous influence in prompting me to take off my mask and let people see the real me.

He is also one of my biggest triggers, but we will get to that.

I met Griffo in London in 2008. We were having a house party and I was living with his bestie at the time. At our first introduction, he walked in on me doing a number two. We laughed and introduced ourselves and then he stayed in the toilet chewing my ear off, while I just sat there wondering when I was going to finish my poo. If you know Griffo, or James, my husband of four years, then you would know he loves a chat. As soon as you ask him how he is going, he will tell you from start to finish about his day, without taking a breath. This is what I love about him; you can take him anywhere and he will have no issue chatting to anyone.

I'd love to tell you that we fell in love at first sight and then lived happily ever after, but that is not what happened next. After this toilet encounter, we did head back to the party and talked all night and did end the night with a party pash, but that was where it ended.

We both spent the next five years doing our own thing. We stayed in touch and messaged one another occasionally; funnily enough we both hooked up with each other's mates during those years.

Fast forward to 2013, when we caught up at our bestie Crombie's thirtieth birthday party. I was on a self-imposed man ban, after hooking up with the wrong guys, too many times. I had also just recently shut the door forever on my very first love, Patty. Patty called it quits in 2013. I was heartbroken at the time, not because we were still in love but because I thought we would always be friends. I honestly thought we would grow old together as best mates because that was a promise we made when we were 19. I think we both always had the door slightly open for one another, in case it didn't work out with anyone else. Well, I know that was the case for me. He felt safe for me. He felt like home. But, he just didn't want the same things in life as I did. I'm grateful he chose to close the door because if he didn't, I wouldn't have been ready for my one true love, who I broke my man-ban for, James Griffiths.

I slept with Griffo in a spa on the first night we hooked up. There was nothing romantic about our drunken shenanigans other than it was so fun and a night I will remember forever. And now our son will too.

After our steamy spa sex, we hooked up for the rest of the weekend. I remember thinking that this felt different to anything

I had ever experienced before. I felt a certain peace within myself, and us. He was treating me like his girlfriend in front of everyone, even when we were sober.

When it was time to leave, I remember thinking to myself, 'Oh, that was so fucking nice, but he will never ask for my phone number!'

I had given up all hope of a guy wanting more than just being my mate or having sex, so when he asked for my number, I almost passed out.

After this epic four days with friends and hooking up with my 'mate' Griffo, I went back to my new life and job in Newcastle, but something was different. I felt giddy … and excited that there might be something more with Griffo. But after a few days of not hearing a thing from him, I put him in the same box as every other guy.

Then the vicious merry-go-round started up: 'Did you really think he was going to call? Who are you kidding? You're so fat, why would he want to date the fat one? You are so not good enough for him.'

I felt sad. I couldn't believe he was like every other guy. I couldn't believe I allowed myself to think for one second that he might be into me and that a fairy tale could exist.

It was the following Saturday night, one week since our steamy hook-up, and I was just about to go to bed after feeling sorry for myself all week when I received a text message from a random number. I had just declared for the hundredth time to my bestie that I was going back on the man-ban, and this time no-one could break it.

I opened up the text. It was Griffo.

My heart was almost pumping out of my chest and my tummy was full of butterflies. I couldn't believe it. He was asking me why I hadn't messaged him back on WhatsApp. Who the fuck messages someone on WhatsApp? It was 2013! He thought I was fobbing him off.

We texted back and forth for hours that night. It didn't stop after that; we literally messaged every minute of the day and if we weren't messaging, we were talking on the phone or on Skype. I will never forget telling my bestie, after a few weeks of this, that I'd met the one. I knew it, I could feel it. Three months of talking 50,000 times a day, he got on a plane and came to Newcastle and the moment he stepped off the plane, I knew my life was never going to be the same and I had found my soulmate.

I cry every time I think about our love story, because Griffo has guided me through some pretty rough times and grounded me into the person I am today.

He has pulled me off the floor in some of my darkest moments and I am forever grateful for the lessons he has taught me and for loving every part of me. This is the most wonderful thing about my husband: he is the definition of unconditional love. He has never ever put conditions on our relationship or me. He has loved me through every path I have chosen to take; he is the one who guided me home to loving myself just by how he loved me.

I wrote this note to him and other partners of mental health sufferers back in 2016, when I first started to speak openly about my anxiety, and I want to share it. Maybe you can share it with your loved ones too.

FINDING MY LOVE WITH MY LOVE

To all partners, friends and family members of those suffering from mental health issues,

Firstly, thank you for all you do, I know sometimes we are a lot to handle, and it can be very frustrating, so from the bottom of our hearts thank you!

I know at times it can be really tough, but we are super grateful that you stick by us.

Living with or supporting a person with mental health challenges can be a very rocky road and there are times that I think you don't really understand us, so I wanted to put together some tips and insights to help us grow.

When I go quiet and withdraw from a situation or a conversation, my energy might come off like I'm pissed off but please know I AM NOT! I am stuck on some kind of merry-go-round of negative thought – I am not just being an arsehole! I promise.

If I am scared, worried or uncomfortable in a situation or conversation, sometimes anxiety will look like anger. I can come across as aggressive, short, agitated and occasionally I might even snap.

Again – this is not your fault. Please try not to react to me!

I can't always tell you when I am about to have a panic attack. Sometimes you'll see physical symptoms like sweating, shaking and my eyes will be wired, other times it's all internal so you won't necessarily see.

If this happens, please just comfort me. I don't need you to react too or give me tough love, I just need you to hold me.

What is going through my head probably is irrational but at that moment, to me, it's very REAL. All I need you to do is listen, see and feel me.

I already feel like a burden in our relationship. I am very aware that you're supporting me and doing your best but if fight or flight kicks in and I become withdrawn and snappy ... I am NOT upset at you and trying to ruin your day.

Please check in with me, don't YOU start acting strange too, that's a recipe for disaster.

We are surrounded by triggers, and unfortunately YOU are one big one. It's not personal, it's just the harsh reality.

Triggers can be conversations, people, situations, one tiny little thing that you or someone did, and it probably doesn't feel like a big deal to most.

Sometimes there is no trigger, and we just wake up feeling like there is a black cloud over us. Some days the feeling will only last for a few hours and other times, it can last days if not weeks.

Thank you for listening and thank you for being our rocks. I know we can be unpredictable, insensitive, irrational and completely detached, so we are forever thankful you've stuck with us!

Love you x

I HAD LEARNT OVER THE YEARS TO COPE WITH STRESS AND ANXIETY BY DRINKING WINE – I COULD EASILY POLISH OFF A BOTTLE OF RED ON A WEEKDAY.

GIVING UP THE BOOZE

Everybody's got a trigger! We all *do*. Triggers are those things that set off our anxiety like nothing else. Most of us know what our triggers are, even if we ignore them. Most of the time, these triggers are also how we learn to deal with our anxiety. It's a double-edged sword. It both numbs and causes the anxiety, and it's terrifying to think of life without it.

At the end of 2017, I went through some major changes with my career and personal life, and I wasn't coping well. I had people around me triggering my anxiety daily, and I was self-medicating to survive the merry-go-round of savage negative self-talk. I had learnt over the years to cope with stress and anxiety by drinking wine – I could easily polish off a bottle of red on a weekday to take away the pain of what was really going on, because in that moment, the wine truly was helping. Unfortunately, I would wake the next morning and the anxiety would be 10 times worse and so the cycle would continue. I lost all my confidence professionally and the only way I felt like me was when I was party-Heidi or drunk-Heidi.

I was drinking almost every day and then binge drinking and blacking out on weekends to survive. In those moments, the fake confidence made me feel like I was overcoming any challenges. But that was all a lie. I wasn't coping at all. I was just masking the issues. At times, I kept hearing a little voice inside me trying to speak, saying I needed to *stop drinking*, but I kept shutting her out with another glass of red.

It was during this dark time that a friend handed me a book called *A Happier Hour* written by a fellow Perth girl, Rebecca ('Bex') Wellar. I couldn't believe the words that she had written. Reading her book was like I was reading the story of my own life. Bex was a party girl and was always the first one at the bar and the last one to leave. She would constantly black out and forever be hating herself the next day after a boozy night. Her anxiety would peak, and so she would drink more again the next night. It was a cycle and one I could totally relate to.

It had all started to unravel for Bex when she decided to leave the corporate world and follow her dream to be a health coach. She'd still consume several bottles of wine per week, and it was in a coaching session with a client that she realised something had to change. After too many mornings filled with regret and tears, Bex embarked on a three-month sobriety experiment that became a quest for self-discovery and ultimately transformed her entire world. Not only is Bex still sober years later but she has a business called Sexy Sobriety that is helping, coaching and mentoring many others to live the best life possible, sober.

Still in denial myself about my own booze battle, I asked Bex to be on my podcast just before that Christmas. Everything she said I could relate to, and that little voice inside was getting louder and louder, telling me I needed to take a break from alcohol, which was the last thing I was going to do right before Christmas holidays and after the year I'd had.

Looking back at photos from that day, you can see how unhealthy I was and that the booze, anxiety and stress were really taking their toll on me. I was bloated and unmotivated, and my self-care practices had been thrown out the window. During these holidays I had my *aha* moment and realised that alcohol was a major trigger for me, and that it was taking a real toll on my health. After weeks of visiting family and friends and drinking almost every night, I was experiencing severe abdominal pain and sickness. This had been the case for the last few years whenever I drank booze excessively, but I was in complete denial despite the mountains of proof. I had severe bouts of gastritis, and it wasn't pretty. At age 20, I'd had my gallbladder removed, and not long after, I had a few complications and was hospitalised for a few weeks with a bad case of pancreatitis. I was told to never drink again. That break from drinking lasted only nine months.

A couple of days after Christmas, the party was still going at my parents' house when I woke in the middle of the night to another bout of severe pain, vomiting and diarrhoea. As I lay on their bathroom floor, Bex's face came to mind, and I realised there and then that I needed to take drastic measures and cut the booze out. It was in this moment that I decided to join her Sexy Sobriety group and give up alcohol for ninety days. I needed this challenge more than ever, and on 8th January, 2018, I made my health the main priority for a change. I can honestly say, sobriety has been one of the most rewarding experiences of my life. I learnt many new things about *me*, and I have tackled things I didn't think I'd have the courage to do without a drink in my hand. When I was sober, I discovered balance. I saw so many benefits in my life, and I had never felt more comfortable in my own skin.

For a long time, red wine had me believe that I was only fun when I drank two bottles of it. Vodka made me feel like my anxiety was under control, and white wine, well ... that was just the devil and I had too many blackouts on the stuff. For far too long, I had numbed my emotions with alcohol, and for the very first time, I had to work through some difficult feelings.

The year 2018 was a massive one for me personally and professionally, which made me feel like alcohol would inhibit some of the big decisions that I had to make. I couldn't have come to this realisation if I was still drinking. It took about 40 days into sobriety for me to realise the power I had within myself to conquer those demons and find that balance I had lost years before. Don't get me wrong, it wasn't a walk in the park. The first month or two was incredibly challenging, especially on social occasions.

People were in shock when Heidi Anderson – the party girl, who was always the first to arrive and the last to leave the bar – stopped drinking.

Some people reacted negatively to my choice to quit booze, and one of the hardest parts was people asking why I wasn't drinking, and the pressure to have 'just one glass of wine'. I'd often hear, 'Go on, it won't hurt you.'

"

WHEN I WAS SOBER, I DISCOVERED BALANCE. I SAW SO MANY BENEFITS IN MY LIFE, AND I HAD NEVER FELT MORE COMFORTABLE IN MY OWN SKIN.

I couldn't believe how much my social life revolved around alcohol. It seems to be at almost every single occasion, whether it's a work function, a lunch date, a night out, or even a Sunday afternoon catch-up. Finding new ways to connect with people and have fun was really tough for me, I had spent much of my life using alcohol to help me connect, but the self-growth far outweighed the shitty moments.

I had plenty of *aha* moments – some of them positive and some incredibly hard to navigate without a red wine in my hand. I had to discover new ways to cope with my feelings. In the past, if I'd had a shit day at work or a disagreement with my partner or a stressful conversation with someone, my go-to would be a few glasses of red to relax.

I also realised, after attending a few events sober, that my social anxiety was what made me drink before every event or occasion. I wasn't as confident as I believed, and the booze gave me a false sense of identity and security. I discovered I was petrified of judgement and small talk. This was hugely apparent to me when I attended a few functions sober. I was in my head the whole time, constantly rushing off to the bathroom to catch a break. At first, I did not know how to deal with the emotions that came up, and I tried to shut them off in the first few weeks with sugar or food. But after my naturopath read me my blood test results, I was told I needed to give up the sugar too.

I truly felt like I was on a wild rollercoaster. I had days where I felt super-overwhelmed with my own thoughts and feelings. I had times when stress was at an all-time high during this period with the loss of a dear mate to cancer and I was putting on my own Love Yourself event. Usually, I would've handled all this with booze and sugar, eating away the stress and drinking away the pain. But I've had to find new coping mechanisms, including one I now swear by: daily meditation.

During this time of sobriety, I learnt so much about myself and became more aware of my true feelings. I felt true happiness on many occasions and natural highs that I thought I only got from alcohol. I became so grateful and happy that I would shed tears of joy daily, even when times were tough. I also experienced sadness and loss in new ways I'd never imagined. Throughout this period, I would often journal these thoughts and feelings, and I came across an entry I would love to share with you:

> Today I'm six weeks sober, 44 days and not one sip, baby!
>
> Sobriety has been by far one of the easiest things I've done.
>
> It's possible for anyone, believe me! I'm a booze hag from way back and your ultimate binge drinker. I could polish off three bottles on my own and party all night; my problem was I couldn't remember half the night and waking anxious was absolutely horrific.
>
> Some Sundays I'd lie on the couch until I had to get up to shower at 8pm at night. These days I'm achieving so much, I have too many hours in the day, exercise isn't a chore and hanging out with mates and having amazing connections has become the norm. Hangovers brought on so much more than a foggy brain; they made me live a lot in fear.
>
> **Decisions made on weekends had been fear based.** I have barely questioned myself this year … I'm definitely going to go longer! I'm just starting to thrive and I'm already halfway.

> I've had time to chase my passions in my spare time, and for that I'm grateful. Seems crazy to think that booze has held me back because for so long it's been a part of me. It helped me when I was sad, it gave me strength when I was in pain, and it made me happy when I was anxious!
>
> Over the last few weeks I've been through a few personal things and health issues and I couldn't turn to alcohol. I really had to sit with my emotions! That has been so interesting.
>
> I have had to cut sugar and carbs from my diet for health reasons also, so this week when I was confronted with a few things, I had nowhere to turn. My security blanket and amazing fiancé is in America, the food I normally ate to comfort me wasn't there, and the booze was a big NO. I felt things I hadn't before, and I saw things I didn't know existed in me!
>
> Fuck, mind blown, hey, I took my spiritual meditation deeper than I ever have and I have explored part of my personality that I didn't know about!

And then another breakthrough!

Four-and-a-half months into my sobriety journey, I had my biggest breakthrough after drinking four wines on a work trip to London. I had lived in London previously and hadn't been back for a few years, so I was extremely emotional about heading back. The day I broke my sobriety, I had many thoughts and feelings running through my mind, but feeling like a failure was the big one.

Looking back, I think my mind was already made up about drinking that day. I just had to prepare myself for the after-effect of the feelings I thought I would have. I had planned to hang out with some of my closest mates, and as it was a special occasion, so I felt okay about trying a drink.

“

AFTER FOUR-AND-A-HALF MONTH'S BOOZE FREE, I FINALLY FELT LIKE MYSELF AND TRULY CONNECTED TO WHO I WAS AS A PERSON.

I hadn't seen my mates in two years, and I was excited but nervous because old Heidi didn't know how to stop drinking with them in the past. I'd gone out with them many times when I lived in London, and back then I had no control. One drink would always turn into a bender and me blacking out. So, all these memories were running through my head on that Friday morning before I met up with them.

I spent all morning thinking about whether I truly wanted to drink, and how I would feel after and I decided, I really wanted to do it. I meditated on these thoughts, and I phoned home to chat with a couple of my closest mates to talk through my exact thoughts and feelings. After a couple of hours of these chats and some meditation, I realised that I wanted to have a drink because I was happy, and I wasn't trying to escape anything. I just wanted to have a drink with my mates, and celebrate our time together, and drink to friendship. I had just ticked over four and a half months and I was ready to find out if I could stop after a couple.

I have always been an extremist, so when I was assessing how far I'd come, I realised that the real challenge for me was to know when to stop, if I had a drink or two. My biggest challenge lay ahead that day. If I was going to drink again, I needed to know when to stop and not go crazy and try to control my drinking – something I'd never, ever done. I have rarely been able to stop after just one glass, so I meditated on this just before I left, and this is what happened next …

That day I had four drinks over eight hours. The first was tasty and I really enjoyed the tiny little buzz. I then had a second glass about an hour later, and that made me feel out of control. So,

I had some water and tried to sober up before dinner. Then, feeling anxious, I automatically ordered a glass of red with our meal to take away the thoughts, and I regret that. I was following the crowd and using an old coping mechanism to deal with my emotions. I then had one more just to top it off after dinner. On the way home I felt disappointed, sick and not like myself at all. I sat in the cab on the way home feeling awful, so I decided to write down what was running through my head. It was at this moment that I realised I really liked myself better, without alcohol, and I would prefer to eat dark chocolate than have a glass of wine.

After four-and-a-half month's booze free, I finally felt like myself and truly connected to who I was as a person. I know this will sound crazy to someone who has never had time away from alcohol, but your clarity when you have no alcohol is just next level. Don't get me wrong, I was happy and pumped to try a nice glass of red, but as I said, after four drinks I didn't feel like me.
I woke up the next day and the booze blues were like nothing I had ever experienced before. I couldn't believe how lethargic and sad I felt after four glasses. The old me could knock back three bottles. Times had definitely changed. I started beating myself up because that was an old habit too, and one I am still very good at, so I meditated on it – that's the new me – and something I suggest you try if you want to connect with the real you. What I realised the next day was I'm actually glad I drank because it was an amazing lesson.

I now know I am more comfortable in my own skin when I'm sober. For a long time, I felt like I needed booze to feel content and like myself, but I don't. I am happy and comfortable with who I truly am, without the booze! Yes, I still drink, but I have never been out of control or blackout drunk since starting on my sober journey.

The challenge for me now is balance, and I'm managing this, even on special occasions!

The lesson for me: confidence doesn't come in a bottle. It comes from within. If you do find it in your glass of wine, it will only be temporary.

“

CONFIDENCE DOESN’T COME IN A BOTTLE. IT COMES FROM WITHIN. IF YOU DO FIND IT IN YOUR GLASS OF WINE, IT WILL ONLY BE TEMPORARY.

“

I HAD TO TAKE FULL RESPONSIBILITY FOR THE PAIN AND SUFFERING I HAVE CAUSED OTHERS.

MAKING PEACE WITH YOUR PAST

For so many of us, our deepest wound is rejection; that's why it can be so tough to cut ties with others or speak our truth. One of my biggest fears is being rejected and not being liked. One of my biggest regrets is that at times in my life, especially in high school or even primary school, I made others feel rejected. This wound still cuts me deeply. I am sorry for being one of the mean girls at times throughout my life. I am deeply sorry for the way I behaved at times in my past and if I could turn back time, I would do it differently.

A few years ago, when I started putting myself out there publicly on TV and radio, I received a comment on one of my posts on social media from a girl I went to school with. It read: 'Did you also hide behind being a bully too ... because of your body image issues? You were so horrible to go to school with.'

I'm not going to lie; this message took my breath away. I felt my world stop and a crushing pain straight through my stomach. I was struck by immense shame, guilt and embarrassment.

The shame I felt in this moment and the guilt I have carried for the past few years since receiving this message has crippled me at times, and it has been something that I have recently been working through. When you receive a message like this, you have to take the time to reflect and look within yourself. I had to take full responsibility for the pain and suffering I have caused others. And for that I am very sorry.

This shame is only new. When I left high school, I don't remember feeling this way. I thought I ended things at school in a really positive light and I am still friends with many of the girls on Facebook today, so I was hugely taken aback by this message.

After I received this comment on my page, I decided to address it publicly on our radio show and in my weekly column.

> This really made me think about my past and what I was like at primary and high school. Yes, this girl was right – I guess I was a bully.
>
> I went to an all-girls high school in the 1990s – man, it was bitchy. There were around 80 girls going through puberty all in one courtyard. As you can imagine, there were some nasty things that were said and done. I never got to see how boys bully each other, but girls can really be 'mean girls'.
>
> I finished high school in 2001 and to be honest, I've put most of it behind me. But clearly this is still affecting my old classmate – for which I feel awful.
>
> During our school years together, I was constantly referred to as 'the fat, loudmouth'.

> I was picked on by bullies and it was always about my weight, and maybe it's a survival technique, but in turn, I was replicating that on to her.
>
> I'm not making excuses and I'm sure parents and teachers see this cycle over and over.
>
> I was just like any other mean girl; I called people names and excluded classmates from our group if they didn't fit in.
>
> I made people feel like shit because that's how I was feeling.
>
> However, for this I'm sorry. I'm sorry for the things I said at school. I'm sorry for the things I did at school to upset or hurt you or anyone else.
>
> I want to personally apologise to the girls I went to school with who I made feel less than because of my own insecurities.
>
> I'm sorry that I didn't understand at the time what effect my actions had on someone else.
>
> Maybe I was just following the crowd? Maybe I was just being a bitch? To be honest, I will never understand why I chose to act this way and I want to take this moment to apologise to you.

I am passionate about women supporting women today – I'm not proud of teenager Heidi's behaviour, but I cannot change what I did at school or take away the pain that I caused this girl or anyone else. I am deeply sorry for your hurt and if you ever wanted to chat on the phone so I can hear your story and apologise in person, please reach out. My hope by sharing this story is that young people don't make the same mistake as me. I'm proud of the person that I am today, and I wish that I knew then what I know now. Hindsight is a beautiful thing, isn't it?

Since the day Memphis was born, I have always said to him, 'Be kind to others always and be kind to yourself. Never forget that.'

I can only apologise for my past behaviours. I can't change the past, but I can create the future.

“

REMOVING THE NEGATIVE IS ABOUT CREATING BOUNDARIES FOR YOURSELF ONLINE AND IN THE REAL WORLD.

REGULAR AUDITS OF YOUR SOCIALS AND LIFE

Stepping into self-love practices and building my confidence on the daily meant looking at my world from a different perspective. It meant I needed to shut down People-pleasing Polly in order to be kind to myself – to the real me. I conquered my people-pleasing with kindness – to others and to myself. When you start to love yourself, you start to take care of yourself, not just physically but your mind and soul too.

One thing I have learnt on the self-development journey is to ask myself better questions. We spend so much time asking ourselves questions that we cannot control, like 'Why doesn't that person like me?'

Try asking yourself better questions instead:

Am I hanging out with people that drain me?

Am I following people online that bring out my inner demons?

These are the kind of questions I ask myself all the time now and this is one of my favourite things to do. I commit to an audit every few months: removing the negative is about creating boundaries for yourself – online – and in the *real* world.

Let's look at an online audit first. Try deleting and unfollowing people that bring you down online.

I did an online experiment a few years ago and the results spoke for themselves. I wrote down how I felt after seeing some of my favourite people online. I noticed a pattern: I compared myself to everyone I was following and then put myself down. Thoughts like, 'You're not good enough … you'll never be as successful as them … look at what they are doing.' And so on. The thing is, there was absolutely nothing wrong with what they were doing; everything they were achieving was about *them.* Those negative thoughts were all about *me.* So, I unfollowed these super-inspiring beings over a six-week period, and I noticed a difference instantly. In total, there were at least a hundred people or groups that I hit the unfollow button on. This was part of an exercise that Dr Katherine Iscoe (Dr Katherine, Body Confidence Expert) got me to do in one of our private sessions.

I met Dr Katherine just over seven years ago when I signed up to her eight-week body confidence course, *The Forever Approach.* I can honestly tell you that I didn't think unfollowing all these women and groups on social media would have an effect on me at all.

For years, I have been following pages that I found inspirational and funny, which featured body confident and happy women, but I had no idea that some of them were having a negative impact on my mental state. When Dr Katherine originally asked me how I felt about the images posted by these pages I followed on social media, I said I was inspired. That isn't a lie. I really am inspired by these incredible humans! However, when she made me write down my thoughts about five of them as an experiment, I realised people I followed weren't inspiring me, they were sabotaging my progress. I had been scrolling over some of these pages more than 10 times a day and, although their posts impressed me, there were more negative thoughts swirling through the back of my mind than positive ones. I'll admit it, I was jealous! I found myself feeling envious, judgemental, even ungrateful, and I compared myself to *all* of these women. This is when Comparison Cassie became really fierce.

My anxiety was sky high back when I was comparing myself to online friends who worked in the radio industry. What really sucked was one of the girls who I compared myself to hourly as I would scroll through all my social media channels, was one of my good friends. She was achieving great success and I loved watching her grow and flourish, I really did, but when I saw her stuff blow up on socials, I was jealous. My green-eyed monster would spiral, and my Negative Nelly would pipe up, creating a merry-go-round of negative self-talk. In the end I had to hide and unfollow my friend, and I felt so shitty about this. I called her up and confessed to her what I'd done. She totally got it and understood.

Today she is a very successful comedian and her profile is HUGE and I follow her again. I love watching her, and the green-eyed monster is well and truly dead. I am one of her biggest cheerleaders. She was doing nothing wrong. It was all about me, and taking the time to work on myself meant that I could work on quietening my Comparison Cassie.

This exercise helped me understand Comparison Cassie – I became super-aware of her and her behaviour. As Dr Katherine explained to me, it is completely normal to compare these stories to our own, but it's important to give our self-confidence a break sometimes too. She also said:

> *Comparing yourself to others is natural. But while we do it, because we know we will, we must remember to put things into the right perspective.*
>
> *However, putting things into a positive perspective is easier said than done. Just like we need a holiday from work to reset our overthinking brains, sometimes we need to have a vacation from social media to reset what we think about ourselves.*
>
> *We need to reset reality by taking a break and focusing on our own lives instead of someone else's.*

I really did notice that the negativity calmed down, and now the comparing is pretty much non-existent. I now spend more time on social media than ever before, but I do an audit every month.

I ask myself the following questions about the accounts I am following:

> *Does this person or thing bring me joy?*
>
> *Is my negative self-talk appearing with the person or thing?*
>
> *Am I following them because I want them to notice me?*
>
> *What are my emotions when I see this account?*
>
> *Do they bring out the best in me?*

“

I REALISED PEOPLE I FOLLOWED WEREN’T INSPIRING ME, THEY WERE SABOTAGING MY PROGRESS.

Before this experiment, I had an obsession with weight loss and fitness pages that consistently post before and after pictures. At the time, I truly believed they were helping me achieve my goals, but now I see they were hindering my progress. Let me just say that I bloody love these women. It's not about shaming them and what they do, what they look like or what they stand for. I've just decided that I don't need to see them in my social feeds at this point in my life. They have done nothing wrong and it's nothing personal. Some women really are a source of positivity and inspiration. I wish them all the very best, but I need to do what is best for me, so I decided *not* to hit the follow button on them.

Today I don't follow any accounts that show the before and after pictures. I choose to follow accounts that set my soul on fire. This goes both ways! Auditing your accounts on social media is a game-changer, and one I teach now in my online course.

Also, if that means you unfollow me, then go right ahead! I'll miss you but I promise I won't be offended! Remember, right now, it's all about you too.

Another regular audit I do involves the *real* world. Get rid of the shit people in your life!

I know this might come across as really harsh, but get rid of the negative people in your life. It doesn't matter if they are related to you or have been your friend since you were a little kid. If they don't align with you any longer or are bringing you down, then it's time to move on. Even writing this brings up big feelings for me, because of my People-pleasing Polly. She is piping in right now as I write this book, 'Are you sure you want to tell everyone to cut people out of their lives? This will mean people won't like you!'

I lost a lot of friends after I left radio, so I understand the feelings on both sides, but sometimes we have to put ourselves first and that may mean cutting cords.

One of my most favourite quotes of all time is, 'People come into your life for a reason, a season or a lifetime.' It is okay to move on from friends or family that aren't aligning with you anymore. It is hard to cut the cord but once you do the feeling is unbelievable.

I am a people pleaser and I like everyone to like me, which can be hard because that means I let people get close to me who aren't really doing anything for me other than draining me, and then there isn't really anything left for the important friends. I cannot tell you how much happier I am to have moved on from some people that were really draining me. It was big for me to let go of these friendships and I had to have some really uncomfortable conversations, but it was so worth it.

I always felt like I was being judged in their presence and I found it really hard to be myself around them, so I was never relaxed or my genuine self. If someone makes you feel like this, ask the question, 'Are they really my friend?' You deserve better and so do I. And let's face it sometimes we just 'outgrow' friends. And that's actually okay!

I know it's easier said than done, especially if you feel like you can't get away from someone because they are your boss, a parent or someone close to you. I would suggest talking to them and letting them know how they make you feel. If that is out of the question, then try enforcing boundaries. I found my psychologist to be a great help with creating these boundaries and rules as I couldn't escape all the negative relationships at that time either.

So, remember if they don't align with you, support you or see you for who you really are, its time to say, 'Bye Felicia'.

Conquering Negative Self-talk with a Positive Mindset

Self-Loathing Lie #3

I'll love myself when I'm more successful

♥

Self-Loving Truth #3

Success is an ever-moving goalpost.
I deserve to be successful because of who I am now.

“

NEGATIVE NELLY WAS CONSTANTLY TELLING ME I NEEDED TO ACHIEVE AND DO MORE BEFORE I COULD BE HAPPY OR LIKE MYSELF.

NEGATIVE NELLY

It's funny how the majority of us say, I'll love myself when I get to the destination, and that is how I have spent so much of my life. I never could be happy with the journey and Negative Nelly was constantly telling me I needed to achieve and do more before I could be happy or like myself. Nothing was ever good enough for her.

I was making huge steps in my career, being promoted from Bunbury breakfast radio to Newcastle then on to Perth. My friends and family were watching from the sidelines cheering me on, but the negative voice in my head was always there, taking me out of the current moment saying things like, 'You aren't successful until you get to Sydney or Melbourne breakfast radio.' And, 'People will only like you if you say what they want to hear.' 'Don't celebrate your success; you don't want to come across like an egotistical dick.'

Fuck what others think!

For things to change for me, I had to start to believe that other people's opinions didn't matter.

I believed for so long that I would love myself when I achieved my goal and dream of working in breakfast radio in a capital city, but when I got there, the goal posts I set for myself kept moving.

I had achieved a lot in such a short time, but Nelly stopped me from being in the moment and smelling the roses. If we had a great radio show or were successful in a ratings period, Nelly would always chirp in with, 'Don't get too big for your boots. You still have so much to prove. You aren't anyone until you move back to the East Coast of Australia and are famous there. No-one knows who you are in Sydney or Melbourne; you are not successful until that happens.' I placed so much of my self-worth and success on what other people thought of me. I still do that at times with social media, but I am far from that person now. I spent so much time in my own head, beating myself up for not being good enough to be promoted for the next job.

At the end of 2017, my co-hosts Will and Woody left our radio show to move back to Melbourne on another radio station on the national drive slot. This was such a terrific opportunity for the 'boy's' and yet I was devastated – left behind, my mind validating that belief again, that I wasn't good enough.

This absolutely broke my heart and forced me into a such a deep spiral I thought I was going to hit rock bottom again. Thankfully, the self-help, self-care, you're OK Heidi, work I'd been doing for the four years when we were on air together helped me work through the pain.

“

THOUGHTS ARE SUPER POWERFUL, AND I BELIEVE YOU CAN CONTROL WHAT HAPPENS TO YOU WITH THEM, WHETHER IT’S GOOD OR BAD.

YOU HAVE THE POWER TO CHANGE YOUR MINDSET

One of the biggest things that got me through my co-hosts leaving the show was my mindset. I'm not going to lie: this was difficult. After speaking to myself negatively for most of my life, I had to start with baby steps, positive affirmations were my very first practice.

I started leaving little messages written to myself on my bathroom mirror:

You've got this.

You are worthy of success too.

You are enough just as you are.

Fuck what everyone else thinks.

You have nothing to prove.

It sounds a little cheesy, but it actually worked. Over time I started to believe what I'd written the day before. My bestie Mel has always been one of my biggest cheerleaders – we have both been there for one another since we were little kids. We started the positive affirmations on the mirror when we were living together when I spoke out in Bunbury about hating myself. This was one of the first steps I took on my love-yourself journey. She joined in, leaving notes, and together we built up each other's confidence. I still do this today, although the message always stays the same:

Love yourself.
Fuck what everyone else thinks.
You are enough, just as you are.

A lady I was working with handed me a book she swore by called *The Secret*. I loved it and read it in a couple of days. This was when I first started to understand the Law of Attraction. The Law of Attraction is defined as the belief that by focusing on positive or negative thoughts people can bring positive or negative experiences into their life.

I had never really heard much about this at the time nor did I really understand it, but I have witnessed the power of the Law of Attraction first-hand on many occasions now. Thoughts are super-powerful, and I believe you can control what happens to you with them, whether it's good or bad. Think back to a time where everything just seemed to go wrong: you had one bad thing happen and then you view everything in a negative light and then it's one thing after another – it goes from bad to worse.

I also have a visualisation board and a gratitude wall. These are hung up in my cupboard so, that whenever I get dressed, I see my goals and repeat my positive affirmations. The gratitude wall is a reminder for me to be grateful for everything that I already have. You should start one too; just remember to show gratitude for things about yourself also, as it's easy to forget and focus on everyone else.

"

IT'S IMPORTANT TO INVEST IN SELF-DEVELOPMENT PROGRAMS – YOU CAN CHANGE YOUR MINDSET AND LIFE FOR THE BETTER.

INVEST IN AND INSPIRE YOURSELF

Invest in yo'self – read, educate and inspire yourself through books, YouTube videos, workshops and self-development programs. When I first started in the radio industry, I was full of confidence and ready to tell jokes and laugh every morning. I had no real ambition to change the world, I just wanted to have fun. It was my dream for years, and then in 2011, I was offered my very first breakfast radio job in Bunbury at Hot FM, now known as Hit FM. I remember thinking this was going to be the best thing that ever happened to me, and I would be lying if I told you, it wasn't. But over my almost ten-year career there have been some tough times.

I am not writing about this for you to feel sorry for me; I'm telling you because I have learned so many lessons along the way and made changes to my mindset that may be able to help you in similar circumstances. I honestly didn't realise how much working in the public eye would affect my confidence and self-esteem. You see, I always thought I had my shit together and didn't care too much what people thought of me. Well, how wrong was I? Working in the public eye and gaining a profile opened a can of worms I'd been hiding for a very long time. My confidence was fake and I was full of self-doubt, and that was intensified by the industry I had chosen to work in. In radio, you are not only expected to share your life, your personality and some of your deepest secrets, but you are sometimes criticised for it.

Radio has changed a lot over the years. Back in the day, people would only know you through the sound of your voice and occasionally see you on the TV, but these days many announcers and hosts have social media attached to their show and their own personal brands. So, you have instant feedback. This can be good and bad.

It's a great insight into what your listeners want, love and hate, but it's hard when they are critiquing your personality. And let's be honest, everyone has an opinion online.

We also got feedback from bosses, teammates, producers, or anyone in the building really. It's supposed to be constructive, but sometimes it can be tough, especially when you are just starting out and it's about your personality. Back in the Bunbury days, we were air-checked by our boss every day – this means listening to parts of the show and deconstructing the content, you as a performer, your personality, and the way you have said things.

I know, I chose the industry, but it was still tough to hear and take in at times. The hardest part for me was learning that people didn't like me. I think that's when People-pleaser Polly really came into her own. Many people laugh when I tell them I lack confidence, because on the radio, I was quite loud, opinionated and outgoing. I worked hard to overcome and tackle some of these demons, using an excellent network of people I have met, along with my friends and family

It's important to invest in self-development programs – you can change your mindset and life for the better through self-development, and that's something I am now super-passionate about.

I have put together a list of the things I have done over the years that have helped me change my negative mindset and helped with my anxiety and performance at work because I saw it as a long-term investment into my mental health and personal growth.

There is NO excuse these days, with access to anyone and everyone online. All you have to do is jump on Instagram and you will find your person. Investing in me has by far been my greatest investments. For the past 10 years, I have attended workshops and completed online programs all while wearing my PJs. I get it. I know how hard it can be, stuck on the loop of self-doubt; I have been there many times before.

I was questioning myself every day and the decisions I was making around my career. For the year after my co-hosts left, I took the time to complete programs and work on my mindset, and the work hasn't ever stopped.

My life did change for the better; not because they left but because I was finally free from the victim mentality. I blossomed in the workplace, and the negativity slowly but surely disappeared. I wouldn't say I was perfect – I am still growing every day – but I can handle situations with so much more ease and clarity.

The panic attacks before and during our radio show stopped too.

IF OUR BRAIN ISN'T FUNCTIONING PROPERLY AND WE AREN'T FEELING OURSELVES, WE SHOULD GO TO A PSYCHOLOGIST, COUNSELLOR OR A COACH.

DATE YOUR PSYCHOLOGIST

Finding a psychologist can be a lot like dating: you might need to try a few before you find the one you connect with. It took me years to find 'the one' and once I did, I have not left her side, and we've been seeing each other for over five years.

Meeting a psych for the first time can be daunting and nerve-racking: you might be very closed off to the first meeting and feel no real chemistry, so I would suggest applying the three-date rule. If after three sessions with a psych you have no connection and aren't getting anywhere, I would suggest looking for a new one. Don't let a few sessions with someone that you didn't really like put you off seeking support or therapy. I wouldn't be where I am today without my psych because mine literally saved my life and its been a huge part of understanding myself and my mental health.

Her name is Jane, and she has been an absolute godsend. We connected straightaway, and I saw her every few weeks when I was really trying to work through who I was and where I wanted to be.

Our sessions were lifesaving for me, I spent many sessions crying uncontrollably wondering how I was ever going to move forward, and then other days, I wouldn't talk at all. There is something about Jane, her warmth and kind nature meant I always feel safe. Safe to feel and just be. I could be my authentic self with her and I could show up however I felt and of course there was never any judgement. There were times when it was really dark, that I couldn't even get a word out, I was frozen in fear, but I would still go because sometimes it felt like she was the only one who truly understood me.

We have tried a few different methods over the years to combat my anxiety, as I am very open to trying different techniques. When I was in the thick of it, we used a therapy called eye movement desensitisation and reprocessing (EMDR) and, without getting too technical (Google it), it has really helped me with my anxiety. It was developed in the 1980s to alleviate the symptoms associated with post-traumatic stress disorder (PTSD). Since then, however, it has become a widely used and effective technique for other psychological disorders, including various phobias and addiction.

Over the years I have tried cognitive behavioural therapy a few times, but I have found the best thing for me is talking. I am a deep thinker and I like to analyse and understand why I feel and think the way I do, and this has been a huge game-changer for my progress with Jane.

Just before I married Griffo, my knight in shining armour, in September 2018, we started seeing Jane together every second session, so that we could have a more open and honest dialogue and work through any underlying issues. We are still doing this today, but with a different counsellor, we like to change it up. Our visits have helped Griffo really understand me and my mental illness.

Yes, there is still a stigma attached to seeing a psychologist, but in years to come this will be the norm. Well, I hope it will be, because there is nothing better than sitting in a room, talking out all your problems, and having someone sit there and listen without judgement.

I'll ask you this question: what do you do if you break your leg? The answer is easy, isn't it? You go to a doctor. If our brain isn't functioning properly and we aren't feeling ourselves, we should go to a psychologist, counsellor or a coach.

In simple terms, which I learnt from a psych years ago, imagine we all have a tool belt on; sometimes that tool belt is empty and there are no tools left in the pockets. When you see a psych, they help you fill up your tool belt with tools, so that you can tackle your thoughts, feelings and challenges.

“

MY MISSION IS EMPOWERING WOMEN TO EXPOSE THEMSELVES SO THEY CAN BUILD THEIR CONFIDENCE.

THE SHED YOUR SHIT PROGRAM

I have taken my personal development so seriously that in 2020, I launched my very first self-love and mindset program called 'Shed Your Shit'.

Over 12 months, my Shed Your Shit movement was on three TV shows in Australia:

- On SBS and currently on SBS demand online *What does Australia Really Think About … Obesity?*
- Channel 10's *Goggle Box*
- Channel 10's *Studio 10*

I developed a four-week online program to help people shed their emotional baggage and start living their best life – exactly what this book is all about.

I was blown away by the response: 2500 people signed up to my free ten-day Shed Your Shit Challenge and I launched my program off the back of it. I had wanted to create this course for years, because this is what I needed when I was going through my shitstorms. I love these women, and not just because they signed up for my course, but because of their support for each other and their openness to grow in the squad. A huge part of shedding your shit is being vulnerable and opening up about how you are truly feeling. I ask women to take off their masks and hold the mirror up.

My mission is empowering women to expose themselves so they can build their confidence. Stepping outside your comfort zone is how you build confidence; it's a learnt skill! We can ALL be confident; we just have to have the courage to try something new. You see, confidence is built when you are uncomfortable. This is why I walk around shopping centres in my bra and undies! Not on a regular shopping day but for some very specific and amazing self-love empowering events. (More about that later.)

So many women have joined me along the way and I am so grateful for their support.

I love to cheer them on, to celebrate them, and show these gorgeous souls that anything is possible. I share tools with them through my programs to inspire and fill these women up with things that have worked for me to become the best fucking version of themselves.

Some of the resources I share in my Shed Your Shit program are books, podcasts and videos which are all available online, and are mostly free! YouTube and podcasts are free and there is so much information online with thousands of life coaches sharing their knowledge, tips and tricks. Investing time in my self-development has been a game changer for me and something I tell everyone to immerse themselves in.

Some of the greats I am obsessed with and who have mentored me without even knowing are Oprah Winfrey on her Super Soul Chats, George Bryant, Angie Lee, Tracey Spencer, Hellè Weston, Tony Robbins, Jake Ducey, Mark Manson, Melissa Ambrosini, Lewis Howe, Sarah Knight, Mel Robbins … and the list could go on. Just Google! There is a worldwide web out there. However, if you want to invest in your mental health and mindset, it starts with you.

"

THESE GLORIOUS GODDESSES WALKED THROUGH THE SHOPPING CENTRE WITH ME AND BARED BITS OF THEIR SKIN THAT THEY HAD NEVER SHARED WITH ANYONE.

WALK OF NO SHAME: EXPOSURE THERAPY

Shed Your Shit went viral after seven other women and I walked through a shopping centre in Perth in our bra and undies with our Walk of NO Shame.

What started as a photo shoot for #shedyourshit turned into a peaceful protest of eight women saying, 'Up yours to society's bullshit lies and expectations.'

Let me explain how this all happened.

I was about to hold a Shed Your Shit workshop and I wanted to promote it differently to every other self-love workshop that was on at the time. I had done plenty of beach shoots in my bikini and I also wanted to personally step outside my comfort zone.

If I was teaching others to do this, I needed to lead the way …

Getting a photo in my bikini at the beach or at home was no longer uncomfortable, it was now a way of life. I live in my bikini in summer.

A few weeks before the movement went viral, I was out getting groceries, and the idea came to me that I should do a photo shoot in a shopping centre in my bra and undies because that was completely outside my comfort zone.

It absolutely petrified me.

My brain started going crazy: *Imagine what people would think of you. They will see you in the worst light, cellulite will be highlighted, back flab, your tummy and they will no doubt see your pubes hanging out.*

I stopped these thoughts and said, 'This is exactly why I need to do this.'

The thought of a photo shoot in the middle of a busy shopping centre was fucking crazy and never in my wildest dreams would I ever think I could do this.

First port of call was amazing photographer Chelsea Bates, who shoots some of my Shed Your Shit events and she loved the idea! She also took the phenomenal front cover pic of this book at my other super talented friend Belle Verdiglione's house.

Chelsea and I have been friends since just before Memphis was born; she took my maternity pics and also was our birth photographer. She has literally seen every part of me.

I then used my connections and got on the phone to make a few calls, and before I knew it the date was locked in for a photo shoot in the middle of a shopping centre, at their busiest time, wearing ONLY my bra and undies.

The shopping centre loved the idea.

I asked the girls in my Shed Your Shit program who wanted to do this with me.

They were quiet. Like really quiet. No-one said anything.

Then one of them piped up and said, 'Fuck yeah, I'll do it with you, Heidi.'

Raelene had recently beaten cancer and had numerous operations. She used to weigh herself daily, but she was now loving her body and she was about to join me in the shopping centre!

Then three more screamed, 'YES!'

Yvonne, Bee and Jaz.

These women were only at the start of their journeys, but they were willing to hold my hand and support me in my quest to change the way society sees women and the beauty standards they hold us to.

These glorious goddesses walked through the shopping centre with me and bared bits of their skin that they had never shared with anyone.

This moment was by far one of the best I have ever experienced.

Alana, Rose, Becky, Yvonne, Raelene, Jaz and Bee, I salute you! This chapter is dedicated to you. Thank you for being an inspiration for women all around the world. I know you were scared shitless, your legs shaking, with sweaty hands and boobies, but you did it. You did it for me and you did it for our future children.

Eight women standing up against the bullshit lies that we've been sold and told for years.

We are told daily how to change and edit ourselves by marketing, advertising and people's opinions. Every day we are judged ... judged by others and by ourselves! We constantly tell ourselves stories like ...

Our cellulite is ugly and needs to be fixed.

Our boobs are too small, or uneven.

Our tummies aren't flat enough.

Our legs are too chunky.

These stories are then verified by others' opinions, marketing and bullshit beauty standards on the internet.

And we wanted to put a stop to it, by saying YES to loving and accepting ourselves.

Women have been programmed to believe we are not good enough through TV, marketing, magazines and now social media.

It doesn't matter what shape or size you are; THEY will tell you it's never good enough.

They play into our insecurities ...

They speak to our egos.

They know what works.

They know you'll continue to pay big fucking dollars looking for a quick fix or diet.

I want to remind you again: You have the power to change your mindset!

Unfuck yourself today like these ladies and educate yourself on diet culture. Be who you were before they told you who to be.

Of course, we were shit-scared, full of anxiety and worried about what people would say ...

BUT we did it anyway ...

WHY?

Because this is living. I still remember all of us standing in the boardroom of the shopping centre in our bras and undies, thinking, "are we really about to do this?" I don't think anyone else in the world that day was doing the same thing as us. It felt wild and crazy, and I was so proud of my sisters.

I asked Chelsea to film as well as take photos because I wanted to capture people's reactions.

We were standing outside the sliding doors about to go into the shopping centre. Everyone was huddled up nice and close, then I said, 'Let's do it, gals! Let's show them what we got and be proud of who we are. It's your body at the end of the day, so FUCK what anyone else thinks. They don't know you. They may be inclined to judge because they've been sold the same bullshit lies as you, but within seconds their next thought will arise and they will be inspired by you.'

I continued: 'You know that first thought is usually a judgemental one; well, it's not usually *your* thought. It's what society has had you believe. Ninety-five per cent of people in there will think you are amazing for what you are doing, and that moment of judgement they may have, won't last long. Believe me, you are going to change lives doing this, including your own.

'Let's fucking do this!'

The doors opened and all anxiety disappeared. I was leading the way.

People stared. We waved. I felt like a celebrity on the red carpet. People started to clap and cheer, then all of a sudden as we moved through the shopping centre people started following us; we had members of the public join us! People started grabbing their phones out to record.

We had pics taken everywhere, including on the escalators and out the front on the pedestrian crossing where car horns honked at us! There were hugs from strangers with tears streaming down faces. I will never forget those cheers of pride from the crowds.

It was so much fun; I remember stopping the girls and asking, 'How do you feel?' and their response was, 'Fucking amazing. Everyone is loving it!'

A lady asked us, 'What are you protesting for?' My initial response was, 'We aren't', but then I said, 'Actually, yeah, we are protesting. We are protesting against bullshit beauty standards and saying up yours to society's expectations and impossible-to-reach beauty standards.'

I was fucking proud in that moment because I think, I truly realised what we were doing for others. Rose and Jaz both had their little ones in prams with us, which made me feel even more inspired because this was for them! They are our future.

My phone literally blew up with love and support and my Instagram stories went viral! People were sharing them, and it was the most views I have ever had. You can still go watch this moment: jump on to my Insta @_heidianderson and look for 'Walk NO shame'.

The highlight for all of us was when an older woman named Maggie came over to thank us. She was bawling her eyes out and was a proud mumma bear. She had short grey hair, the most beautiful smile and the bluest of eyes. As we were getting a picture with her, she said, 'You women are so brave. I would so love to join you but what would all these people think?'

I turned to Maggie and said, 'That is exactly why you should take it off.'

We embraced and she said, 'YES, okay!' and started stripping off in the middle of the shopping centre. We were all screaming her name, 'Maggie, wahooooooo, Maggie!' cheering through the streams of tears.

Maggie, a random stranger, took her clothes off in the middle of a busy shopping centre. She was FREE!

That's what it honestly feels like: FREEDOM.

Knowing that no-one's opinion matters except yours is one of the most liberating feelings I have ever experienced.

This is exposure therapy and I promise you that it can change your life. Google it: it's one of the quickest ways you can unfuck yourself. That is WHY I choose to do exposure therapy regularly;

if something scares the shit of me, like wearing bra and undies in a shopping centre, I'll do it.

Exposure therapy is a psychological treatment that was developed to help people confront their fears and can be effective in the treatment of anxiety disorders. According to EBBP. org, about 60 to 90 percent of people have either no symptoms or mild symptoms of their original disorder after completing their exposure therapy.

My friend Jess Keogh is a body positive counsellor and works with exposure therapy. She says, 'You can change your life from exposure therapy. It's really effective. Yes, it's uncomfortable, but like anything, the change comes from the discomfort.'

Living authentically IS feeling all the feels and showing up anyway, as ourselves, with no masks. For far too long, we've given away our power to strangers. And on that day, we put a STOP to that.

We celebrated ourselves for all our beauty, inside and out.

This powerful exercise is a game changer for destroying years of negative self-talk in one walk: 'The Walk of NO Shame'.

This movement is my WHY!

Ten years ago, I couldn't even get my arms out in public.

Five years ago, I wouldn't wear swimmers to the beach without shorts.

Two years ago, I couldn't wear a bikini.

Today ... well, you can see for yourself: just visit my social pages or hit the QR link in the back of the book!

I have never felt more alive or more comfortable and supported than I did in this moment, in my bra and undies.

“

I MADE A COMMITMENT TO STEP OUTSIDE OF MY COMFORT ZONE AND DO THINGS THAT WOULD TEST MY LIMITS.

SAY YES: STEP OUTSIDE YOUR COMFORT ZONE

SAY 'YES' to everything and push yourself out of your comfort zone. Anxiety is a bitch and at every opportunity Anxious Annie will rise up and try to stop you from living your best life. For far too many years I let my anxiety rule every decision I made. I think that's why most of my crazy decisions were made under the influence. After I opened up about my anxiety and I started to heal, I decided I needed to say yes to more things. I made a commitment to step outside of my comfort zone and do things that would test my limits while pumping some adrenaline through my veins.

I used to play things safely, unless I was drunk, and never really stepped out of my comfort zone. (Well, I did step outside of my boundaries when I entered the *Big Brother* house.) I would always think the worst about a situation. I refused to go skydiving twice in the past because I was almost certain my parachute wouldn't open but in my 'yes' year in 2016, the opportunity arose again and I did it, and it was by far one of the most exhilarating things I have ever done in my life. I'll never do it again, but I did it.

I'm not a big fan of change. I wouldn't even attempt to drive home a different way, just in case something bad happened, so when I decided to go skinny-dipping with a thousand other people, my friends thought that I'd lost the plot. I got completely nude, along with almost a thousand others, and it was a surreal experience. It was probably one of the most random, scary, fun, outrageous, liberating things I've ever done. The feeling was electric. It was a day of strongly felt emotions, waiting in the registration line, you could feel the nervous tension bouncing off some people, while others had excitement oozing out their pores.

The buzzing feeling on the beach, minutes before we all stripped off, was something I'd never, ever felt before. The moment I took my sarong off, I had an intense feeling of vulnerability. But that quickly left when one of my girlfriends grabbed my hand and we ran to the water together. We were free! Swimming in the nude with all those strangers was great fun and I highly suggest you do it sometime. We broke the world record for the biggest skinny-dip. But the best part about the whole experience for me was shedding some of the bullshit surrounding my negative body image issues that I'd carried around with me for years. My favourite thing about it was watching people from all different walks of life celebrate and embrace who they were as people.

I also said YES to couples' nude yoga. Yep. You read that correctly. Nude yoga. As a couple. With other couples. My friend Rosie Rees creator of 'Naked Awakening' ran the class with her partner at the time and they had told me so much about it and its benefits for relationships. Rosie explained, 'The class is essentially about conscious non-sexual intimacy and incorporates breath-work, meditation and partner yoga stretches in order to bring partners into ultimate presence with each other.'

I was very nervous going into the class. I trusted them and their profession, but there were still so many scenarios running through my mind. *What if Griffo gets a little too excited? Where do I look? What if I laugh? What if I don't look sexy? OMG my stomach; what if he notices all my rolls? What if it turns into an orgy? What if I fart? Oh, no, what if I get my period? How intimate will this get?*

Not one of my concerns became a reality. The class was nothing like I had envisioned. When we first arrived on our mats, we were still wearing our dressing gowns.

We sat cross-legged facing each other and we began the class staring into each other's eyes for what felt like forever. This part is what I found the most uncomfortable and we were still fully clothed. I was 100 per cent exposed in that moment and I wasn't sure how I felt about it. I could feel him looking deep into my soul. No words were exchanged, we just had to stare. I continually gave him this cheeky, weird smile. My cheek trembled the entire time. I was completely out of my comfort zone. Staring into someone's eyes is tough.

After a few minutes, Rosie asked the ladies to turn around so our backs were facing the men. They then had to slowly undress us while massaging, tickling or rubbing our backs. This moment was special and very, very sexy. If we were alone, I think we both would've been at it. Once starkers, the couples faced each other and we sat butt naked in the candlelit room, excited but nervous about what would happen next. It was in this moment that I let go of all my hang-ups and worries. I embraced being without my protective armour (my clothes) and came to the moment with my love. I really enjoyed what we did next; as a couple we attempted many yoga positions, even the downward dog. Some positions were romantic and made me feel really content in our embrace, and others were just exciting and fun.

Once you get over the initial fear of being naked, it's extremely liberating. For the last pose, I had to pretty much straddle Griffo. I'm sure there is a technical term for this, but I've forgotten it for now. But this moment was truly special. I felt a deep connection. The energy between us was extraordinary. Our hearts were touching, and we whispered special somethings into each other's ears. I felt secure and content. I was truly happy in that moment.

I still to this day do nude yoga with my soul sister Rosie Rees, she has played a huge role in my quest for confidence and self-love and I am forever grateful for what she has given me.

“

MEDITATION ALLOWS YOU TO WATCH YOUR THOUGHTS AND NOT RUN AWAY WITH THEM OR FROM THEM.

MEDITATE TO FIND PEACE

I first heard of meditation back when I was a kid and my dad was doing it before work to help with his stress. No-one really explained it to me; all I knew was that I couldn't go into the walk-in robe as it would distract him. I think he did it for a few months and then stopped. I wasn't introduced to meditation again until my late twenties when my best friend Mel bought her very first yoga studio. She would run a few guided meditations in some of her classes. I loved the way it made me feel but I would never find the time to do it at home alone.

I don't think my poor little mind had ever felt peace because the first time it experienced silence back in 2016, I cried. It didn't last long but my mind was silent for the first time ever and I loved it.

After feeling that inner peace, I was signed up within 15 minutes of the class ending to a six-week course on meditation run by two monks. This course was one of the best things I have ever done. It was about meditation, its benefits and how it could help me through my anxiety and understand my thoughts.

Throughout these six weeks, I meditated most days up to an hour. It wasn't easy, but I was finding peace. After the course I continued to meditate a few times a week, but slowly as my anxiety started to quieten down, I got lazy and stopped making it part of my routine. I knew how good it made me feel but the excuses came back and I wasn't allowing myself the time. Occasionally I would meditate in a yoga class but that was it.

I noticed a couple of things during this 12-month period: my negative thoughts had started returning again, I was finding it harder to let go of things, my mind wasn't switching off, I was anxious and drinking a lot.

After reading numerous self-help books, I decided it was time to start meditation again. It didn't become part of my routine, but I was doing it three to four times a week and I was noticing the difference. But as life got busy – my meditation would stop.

At the end of 2017 I had started drinking heavily again, there was lots of change happening around me, and my stress levels were at an all-time high. I made a commitment to myself that my meditation needed to become a priority and that it needed to be a part of my everyday routine. This was a non-negotiable. I then went on to meditate every single morning before my radio show for five to 10 minutes in a dark and empty space. After I exercised on the weekends I would stretch and find 10 to 15 minutes to meditate and check in with myself. Before bed I would commit to 10 to 15 minutes also.

Today, with a toddler, my meditation practice is a little different again. I try almost every day to get a 10-minute meditation in but sometimes that can be impossible. I have learnt a lot about myself through meditation, but the number one reason I keep meditating is it makes me feel more grounded, less stressed and happier.

For those new to meditation, let me give you a few tips that I have picked up over the years. Meditation is the training of your mind to focus on the present moment. Meditation allows you to watch your thoughts and not run away with them or from them. Think of it as a training session for your mind; every time you meditate you are growing stronger. You are learning to be present with how you really feel with no distractions. Our emotions can't go anywhere until we deal with them and we can do that through meditation.

My favourite analogy for meditation, which I was taught when I very first started, and I preach whenever I am trying to convince someone to try it, is to pretend you are at a train station and you are standing on the platform. The trains are your thoughts. Stop and watch them pass you by but don't get on the train. If you accidentally take the train, jump off at the next station. It's that simple. You are trying to create distance and an awareness around your thoughts. We all run off at times with different trains of thought, but the key is to detach and get off the train.

Finding a meditation to suit you might take time and you might have to experiment with different styles and that is totally okay. I sometimes sit in silence and use the techniques that I learnt from the monks, and on other occasions my busy little baby brain is called to listen to a guided meditation. Guided meditations are everywhere, and you will find thousands on YouTube. I also use a few meditation apps:

- Insight Timer
- Headspace
- Calm
- Pure Mind
- Mindfulness App

You don't even need to create a space for meditation. You can do it anywhere, anytime. Some people like to set up space in their house and that is cool too. Some people sit and others lie down, like me. I find it really uncomfortable to sit for too long. You have to find what works for you; there is no right or wrong. Just find some time to create this space in your life. You could even do it in your car before or after work. You have to find what works for you and stop with the excuses; I promise it will benefit your life.

IT'S ESSENTIAL TO TAKE TIME OUT FOR YOUR MENTAL HEALTH WHEN YOU NEED IT.

TAKE TIME OUT FOR YOUR MENTAL HEALTH

Did you know two in five Australians aged 18 – 85 had experienced a mental disorder in their life, according to ABS in 2022. The more we speak out about mental health and start conversations, the less alone people will feel. Mental health is something we can take for granted and it's a topic that can make many of us feel uncomfortable, but this shouldn't be the case. So, let's keep this conversation going by being open and honest about how we are truly feeling.

Take a mental health day if you need it. If you need to have time off for your mental health, don't be afraid to take it. I've had to do this in the past and it has helped clear my head tremendously. When my anxiety was at an all-time high and my co-hosts were leaving, I had to take a couple of days for my mental health.

I can understand why people are afraid to speak up and say they need to take a mental health day, as there still is a stigma around the topic. I was so worried that my team and our listeners would think I was weak. I get told all the time how strong I am, and I didn't want to let others down, but I needed to put myself first and take a breather on a couple of occasions. Trying to put on a fake smile or pretending to laugh is an exhausting thing to do, whatever job you do. I had done it plenty of times before and that's what sent me into my anxiety meltdown, so I am grateful that I took some responsibility. It's essential to take time out for your mental health when you need it.

I struggled to get out of bed one morning, but I did, and I got to work before the show. However, in the planning meeting, I could barely get a sentence out. I wasn't feeling great, or like myself at all, but I kept on pushing through. My body felt weak and my energy was at an all-time low. At 5.45am, 15 minutes before our microphones were turned on to do our radio show, I burst into tears. I could barely get my words out and I was in a panic, with irrational thoughts racing through my head. I was thinking, *I can't pretend to be happy on the radio, people will know I am a fake. How can I fake laugh when I can barely speak?* I was trying to get my shit together, but I just couldn't. Everything that came out of my mouth was nonsense. Our producers tried to comfort me, but everything I had been holding in for the past couple of weeks was just flooding out in tears. They tried to send me home, but I felt like I was letting the whole team down, including our listeners.

I thought, *I can't take a day off work just because I am not happy! What will people think?* I was afraid people would think I am weak and that I didn't deserve this job.

About two minutes before we spoke on air, I burst into tears again. I called my boss and she said, 'It's just one day, Heidi.' She assured me no-one would think I was weak and that no-one in their right mind would think I had let them down. I was embarrassed and felt ashamed, but I walked out of the studio that day, turning my phone off as I left. I slept and ate some soup (okay, that's a lie, I ate lots of chocolate), and the next day went into work feeling like a new person.

Why was I so afraid to be open and real? I think I judged myself more than anyone else that day and that's why I encourage you to take the day off if you need it for your mental health. I ask bosses to support their staff, just like mine did. There was no judgement; she just comforted me.

If you need a day or two, take it. Your health is what keeps you alive.

Conquering Anxiety with Self-Acceptance

Self-Loathing Lie #4

I'll love myself when I feel worthy

♥

Self-Loving Truth #4

I am worthy the way I am now and need to let others see the real me

“

BEING VULNERABLE IS NOT A WEAKNESS BUT A SUPERPOWER – A SUPERPOWER THAT I WANT OTHERS TO KNOW THEY HAVE TOO.

OVERCOMING THE ANXIETY MONSTER

Opening up on the radio in 2012 and 2016 has by far been the best thing I have ever done for my personal growth. What I have since realised – is that being vulnerable is not a weakness but a superpower – a superpower that I want others to know they have too. I have made it my mission to share and be vulnerable on a daily basis, through blogs, online columns and my social media. Speaking my truth has been a huge part of the healing. For a very long time I didn't believe I was worthy of happiness, love or even success.

Over the years, I wrote about mental health every opportunity I had, and how the power of speaking my truth has by far been one of my greatest gifts I have ever given myself.

Nearly a decade on from my confessions and numerous therapy sessions later, I now say I experience anxiety on occasions. I am not my anxiety and it does not define me.

Yes, being vulnerable is the first step to taking your power back, but you must put effort in daily to quieten Anxious Annie's voice and overcome the Anxiety Monster.

During those few years post-*Big Brother* and around the time I opened up, I had absolutely no confidence and it has taken years to build it up.

It takes daily work to tackle anxiety and build confidence, and one of the most impactful ways I have been doing that is by making 1 per cent changes. If I make a 1 per cent change every day, in one year's time I have made 365 per cent! When you think of it like that, you think, 'Fuck yeah, that's so achievable!' Don't you think?

I chose to tackle my anxiety through all different avenues and some of these are the little 1 percenters'. Here are a few examples you can try.

Get out in nature. I have a confession; I am a tree hugger. I know some of you might laugh, my hubby does! Almost every day I hug a tree. I find it to be so calming and grounding. Almost daily, Memphis and I head to the beach before 9am. This is our time to connect with ourselves, nature and each other. I aim to get outside a couple of times a day, just to breath in the fresh air and stare at the sky. This is mindfulness and I promise you will feel more at peace if you can implement nature into your day.

And, of course, it's your choice if you hug that tree!

Turn your phone off regularly. I turn my phone off every night now and I don't have it in the bedroom either. By 7pm it's on flight mode and it's not on first thing. What's the first thing you do in the morning? If you're like most people, you wake up to the alarm on your phone, check socials and/or emails, and within minutes your anxiety is fuelled by what you have just read. You have a choice! I choose to turn my phone on around 7 or 8am, once I have done some yoga, meditated, journaled, kissed my son, been outside and had a walk. I fill my tank up first and now I experience less anxiety.

Meditation, as I said earlier, has been a huge help and one that I still need to do more of. I constantly find excuses to avoid sitting in silence, but I am getting there and trying to do it a few times a day because when I do, it works wonders! Yin Yoga at my bestie's yoga studio has encouraged me to check in with myself and switch off, to seek that peace my brain struggles so hard to find. I have dōTERRA oils burning in the house and I wear an oil called Balance every day. Some people may find this really woo-woo, but I guarantee it has helped me! I read lots of articles and books to educate myself on mental health. I also realise that everyone has different experiences and different ways of finding that solace, quieting down those voices, and taking back their lives. So, you do you, babe!

I openly share my story now and speak at events, even though this does cause some anxiety, but I figure I am allowed to have it as I'm speaking about anxiety. So, it's a guaranteed laugh at the beginning!

Make a start with a 1 per cent change, that's it! Then you are already winning.

THE VOICES WERE GETTING REALLY LOUD AND AGAIN I FELT LIKE I WAS A STRANGER TO MYSELF.

MY ANXIETY GOES PUBLIC ON *BIG BROTHER*

I don't really talk about my *Big Brother* experience because I felt so much shame and anxiety when I left 'that' house. I was so bloody happy to be evicted because I was so unhappy in there my last week; I was not myself at all, and that was broadcast to the whole of Australia. It has been nine years this year since the experience, and I have never watched an episode. I have seen a highlights reel, and that was enough for me … Maybe one day I will watch it and laugh.

The shame I felt daily after the show went on for a very long time. It took years to appreciate, love and accept that I did my best, and to embrace the experiment and not beat myself up for it.

I get asked a lot, 'Why did you do it then?' When I tell people it was on my bucket list and something I wanted to do since watching the show as a kid, they always laugh and say, 'Never in my life would I do such a thing!'

I auditioned for years and years from when I was in my late teens; for some reason, I was craving fame and thought this is what I wanted.

At 29 years of age when I entered the house in 2013, that's no longer who I was. It was just that I'd auditioned so many times, I thought, *I need to prove to these fuckers they should put me in there!*

I met some incredible people and created memories I will never ever forget. But at that time, I wasn't really self-aware and I was uneducated about anxiety.

Yes, I had been diagnosed in 2009, but what I didn't understand was that it didn't just go away. I honestly thought after completing my sessions with a psych that I was cured. I also thought the way my brain was wired was the same as everybody else's ...

The *Big Brother* house was by far one of the toughest things I ever did. I changed in there for the whole of Australia to see. I felt it but didn't know or understand myself enough to explain what was happening. I went in there this happy, bubbly, life-of-the-party, positive girl and by the last week, I was negative, snappy and unhappy, as I was a confused soul. I didn't know what was happening to me.

The voices were getting really loud and again I felt like I was a stranger to myself. I will never forget one of the producers saying to me the day after I was evicted: 'You weren't the person in there that we thought you'd be.'

That triggered a vicious cycle of insecurity, shame and embarrassment, and these words went over and over for months, even years!

I had let them down, and I had let myself down. I beat myself up for so long. In hindsight, I wish I knew then what I know now because I would've asked back then, 'What do you mean?'

And then gone on to explain the way my brain works when it's anxious. I become cold. Sometimes the fear made me angry. I became reclusive, and I could be very abrupt. Some days I felt unmotivated, and I was constantly overthinking anything anyone said to me in the house.

'It's time to go, Heidi …'

That producer was right, though – I wasn't myself.

I was out of my comfort zone, and all I could think about was what everyone else thought of me. I wish I could've educated the public on anxiety but I had no idea myself at that stage, what it really was, and how it was affecting me daily. People just thought I was a moody bitch at the end. I wasn't … I was an insecure, frightened people-pleaser who wanted to appease everyone: producers, housemates, and the public.

Once I was evicted, the social anxiety skyrocketed.

No-one knows this except the person I stayed with after the show, but I couldn't get off the floor of his spare room for three days. I couldn't go home, talk on the phone or see anyone because I was so empty and embarrassed by what that producer had said to me. I tried to avoid watching the show, using social media and reading comments and articles about me.

I was judging myself enough; I didn't need to know how the public was judging me too.

I am grateful for the opportunity, and I did honestly have some of the best times of my life.

Yes, I said and did things I regret, but I am only human, and I am thankful for the friendships I made during the experience.

And after almost nine years, it feels good to get that off my chest!

"

I TAKE A BREATH, AND THEN IT'S ALMOST LIKE SOMEONE LIFTS THE CURTAIN TO REVEAL A NEW PERSON AND I SEE WHAT THEY ARE SEEING.

SEEING SOMEONE ELSE IN THE MIRROR

On the 28th of September, in 2018, I married the love of my life, Griffo, at Chandeliers on Abbey in Yallingup, in front of 130 friends and family. I felt a million bucks in my wedding jumpsuit and rocked it with champagne confidence as I pretty much ran up the aisle.

But when I first tried on the jumpsuit, I hated what I saw. When I first looked at myself in the mirror I froze, and I saw someone else. This isn't the first time this has happened or the last. When I saw the photos taken for this book, the exact same thing happened.

Have you heard of body dysmorphia?

It's defined as 'a mental illness involving obsessive focus on a perceived flaw in appearance. The flaw may be minor or imagined. But the person may spend hours a day trying to fix it. People with this disorder may frequently examine their appearance in a mirror, constantly compare their appearance with that of others and avoid social situations or photos.'

The day I tried my jumpsuit on, I saw someone else in the mirror, and I panicked. It went like this: I was triggered as soon as I looked in the mirror; all of a sudden, the person looking back at me was someone else. She was overweight, unattractive, and her hair didn't suit the outfit. In this moment I became obsessed with my hair. I refused to look at my body any longer and I focussed on my hair. This has always been the trigger for me; it happened at my school ball.

My heart races, the thoughts in my head get really loud, and it almost feels as if my skull is about to cave in. Nothing anyone says helps.

I spiral, obsessively looking at my hair and picking apart every detail of my body.

Usually, the people around me are baffled, almost feeling like they're the crazy ones as they are not seeing the same thing as me.

An episode like this lasts around 30 minutes.

I cry.

I stamp my feet like a toddler.

I take a breath, and then it's almost like someone lifts the curtain to reveal a new person and I see what they are seeing. I physically felt and saw the switch in my brain flick that day leading up to my wedding. It was a powerful moment and one I will never forget.

“

YOU GET A CHOICE. YOU DON'T HAVE TO HAVE A SHAME HANGOVER. YOU CAN CHOOSE TO THINK DIFFERENTLY!

MY BODY CONFIDENCE BREAKTHROUGH

I had to share this breakthrough with you because, for as long as I can remember, every holiday I have ever been on, I haven't ever truly lived in the moment. My anxiety kept me obsessed in my head to the point where I didn't enjoy the holiday to its full potential. But something happened in 2017 when I got engaged on our road trip: I let all my shit go. That piece of baggage was finally left behind and my God, it felt good! I was finally out of my head and living my life. Who knew it could feel so damn good?

On previous holidays, I was so worried about what I ate and drank, and I counted every calorie. Today, I love holidays. I wasted so many holidays craving routine.

My anxiety would be triggered by food, alcohol and fun.

I would look back at pics of myself on holidays, comparing my waistline to other pics of me on holidays ... this sounds so screwed up when I put this in writing but it's true, it's what I would do. I was comparing how much weight I'd put on. I know! WTF?

I think my psychologist would call this self-sabotaging!

When I would 'let go' I would beat myself up for it. It was a vicious cycle and one I found really tough to break.

I struggled to be in the moment and enjoy my time with my friends and family. If the voices got too loud, and they would after 'losing control', I'd drown them out with more food and drinks.

It was never ending and then … they got louder and louder.

Today, I've found balance; it takes work daily. BUT! I'm happy and you can be too! If your voices are loud after a weekend or a holiday of eating and/or drinking whatever you want, you need to know that the more you focus on what you didn't do the louder they will get!

Life is a gift and if you had a fucking great time and you enjoyed yourself at the time BUT now your Negative Nelly is speaking up, please know you are not alone and you can change the story! Self-loathing Sally loves to drag you back to that unhappy place.

However, you can choose to think different thoughts.

Sally and Nelly don't have to win! Nor should they be allowed to come in and sabotage the great memories you have created. You get a choice. You don't have to have a shame hangover. You can choose to think differently!

If this is you right now, I want you to STOP! Chuck on some Spice Girls and sing your heart out: 'Stop right now, thank you very much.' This is what I do when I am beating myself up. Another favourite is 'Let it Go' from the movie *Frozen*. Can you see me now? Singing with no pants on!

This is where the work comes in; not in the moment but after the glorious memories you've made.

I write about my weight, body image, exercise, food obsession, anxiety and so on. That is because I have believed for so long that this is what defines me and others. Shallow, I know, but it's hard to shake a belief that you created in your teen years. It will take time. Since forever, I believed I'll be good enough when I lose weight, when I'm a smaller size, and so many of my thoughts generally focus on this and that's a shit place to be.

If you've been there, then you'll understand.

So, for the past few years, I've been placing a lot of energy into working through this 'part of me' and trying to get it under control, because, believe me, it's exhausting being so obsessed and constantly worried. But I have seen the light and holy moly, it feels bloody awesome. I had finally experienced a holiday when I didn't feel guilt and shame around what I'd eaten or drank, or the lack of exercise that I'd done. I took one day at a time and enjoyed every single moment. I didn't look in the mirror and see a bloated mess who had drunk far too many reds and eaten too much cheese. I looked in the mirror and felt sexy in my swimmers, every single day, no matter what I'd eaten or drank!

This was truly awesome for me, and I had to share it, to give others hope. I can't tell you how nice it is to feel peace, to finally have those mean girls, shut the fuck up. For so many years, the negativity was just so loud, but now, I'm living, and I'm obsessed with doing that. On that holiday I enjoyed sunsets, going for beach and bush walks, living in a camper, eating chocolate, swimming, drinking champagne – absolutely everything.

I'm still learning and doing my best to 'let it go'.

I love this quote by Fred DeVito, and it sums up so much about my journey. 'If it doesn't challenge you, it wont change you.'

Becoming Me – the Final Chapters

Self-Loathing Lie #5

I was born this way, I can't change!

♥

Self-Loving Truth #5

The world tells you; you can't change. But the truth is, you can!

“

SOMETHING INSIDE OF ME CHANGED WHEN I WAS 30 WEEKS PREGNANT, AND FROM THAT MOMENT ON, I HAVE BEEN AT PEACE WITH MY BODY.

THE REBIRTH

On the 5th of September, 2019, at 4.17pm, it wasn't just my baby boy Memphis who was born; I was too, his mother.

Having Memphis has been the greatest gift, and he has already taught me so much.

When I fell pregnant and had my son, something inside of me changed. I felt a shift, one that I had been on a mission to find for years. I had tried every diet in the book and searched for this peacefulness through every addiction – sex, drugs and booze.

Something inside of me changed when I was 30 weeks pregnant, and from that moment on, I have been at peace with my body. The war I'd been fighting for many years was finally over. Even after I had him by C-section and my entire body had changed, I was at fucking peace with myself. I had fallen in love with my body in a whole new way.

The road to get there wasn't all smooth sailing. In the first few months of pregnancy, I was full of angst and anxiety. I found out I was three weeks pregnant on our honeymoon; I know it was the next step in our relationship. Still, I was shocked and not really prepared mentally for this massive change in our lives. Of course, I wanted to keep the baby, but in the first few months I struggled to talk about the pregnancy with friends and family, even if they knew, because I was finding it hard to come to terms with the weight gain, and the anxiety I was feeling around my identity was causing a bit of a circus in my mind.

I was processing this next chapter and what it meant for us, and the hormones weren't helping. I was in mourning for my identity. The grief I felt about the old me and my life, meant I was unable to focus on the future, until I had let go of the past life. Even finding out on our honeymoon was difficult, because not only was the partying cut short, but I was super-emotional and irrational. Hormonal Heidi is an absolute ball-tearer; please don't ever ask my hubby about this as I don't think he will be as kind.

Old demons came back for me about my body, and I found myself trying really hard to control my calorie intake, all while having all-day sickness for the first 16 weeks. I found documenting my pregnancy journey and my feelings very therapeutic, and one of the best things I could've done because spewing out these thoughts on social media made me feel less alone.

"

LIFE IS TOO SHORT TO BEAT OURSELVES UP ABOUT BACK FAT, FLABBY ARMS OR A BULGING BELLY.

YOUR STORIES GOT ME THROUGH PREGNANCY

At 17 weeks pregnant, I thought I'd better start documenting my baby bump because I'm super-grateful that I get to experience this.

I posted a picture on my Instagram of the barely-there bump, and that took a lot of guts. I did *um* and *ah* about whether to share it because my negative body image issues had been rearing their little heads from the moment, I found out I was pregnant. Believe me, if I could switch that shit off, I would, but it's definitely not as easy as that.

I look at this photo now and wonder 'what the fuck I was seeing in the mirror', isn't it crazy when you look back at photos of when you think you looked a certain way and then seeing it years later you can *see* it with a different perspective. Crazy how the mind works isn't it?

The Insta post:

> I love to share these experiences because one thing I've learnt since I started being vulnerable and sharing thoughts publicly is that I am never alone. I'm comforted by the fact people are or have gone through the same thing.

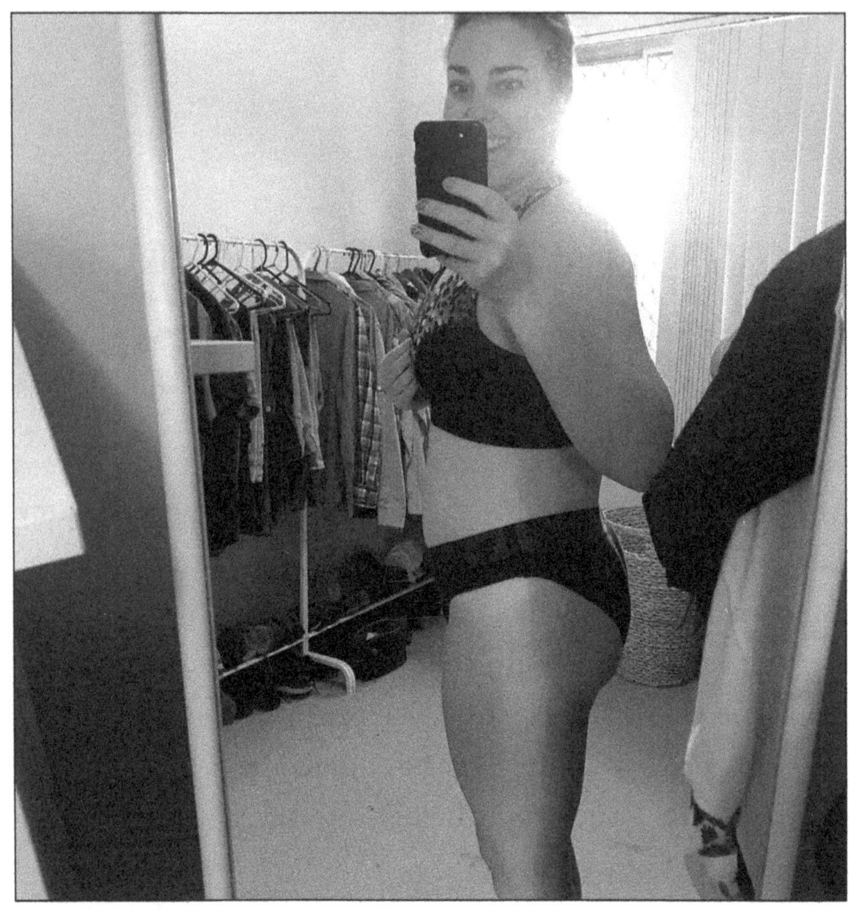

My tummy and arms have always been the area I tend to focus on when speaking negatively to myself, and this is what I've found really hard to switch off lately.

Every time someone said to me, 'Oh, you still have no baby bump,' my first answer was, 'Oh, I know, but I've put on weight in my arms and back.' I keep focusing on this and what I realised yesterday is I'm always giving away my power. I'm not embracing this amazing, beautiful time in my life. So, if you're in a similar headspace, let's fuck these negative thoughts off right now and embrace our bodies for where they are now.

I couldn't believe the number of women who contacted me through Instagram to share their stories of negative body image throughout their pregnancy. Katie's body demons triggered severe anxiety for her through the first couple of trimesters: 'I was overthinking everything, not feeling beautiful, or motivated to get dressed and go out. I had agoraphobia and losing my waist was the huge trigger.'

Carla's weight ballooned uncontrollably throughout her pregnancy: 'My hormones had a mind of their own, and I gained 35 kilos, and it was mostly fluid. I felt like I lost control over my body and how it looked, which for someone who had suffered from an eating disorder in her teens triggered a lot of anxiety.' She introduced Pilates, swimming and walking for her body and mind to help.

Jessie overcame her body issues through pregnancy by seeking help from a nutritionist and researching what foods to eat that would satisfy her hunger. 'My biggest tip would be to research the foods that fill you up and taste great. This way you can have room to indulge in these womb-service moments, knowing you have fuelled your body and your baby. Even jumping on Instagram and following nutritionists and getting free info was a great help.'

I loved Shelley's advice because I feel like we all do this, whether we are pregnant or not: 'I would say, don't compare yourself or your pregnancy to other women. We are all unique and beautiful in our own way, our bodies do different things at different times.'

I asked these women, 'How do we try not to pass these demons on to our kids?' and I loved Shelley's response: 'The most important thing I want my daughter to learn is self-love; the first thing, I ask my partner when I put an outfit on is, "Do I look fat in this?" I need to stop as I don't want her to hear these things.'

Jessica Smith is a great friend of mine and a former Paralympian who is a fantastic advocate and speaker for positive body image. I asked her about her recent pregnancies as she has had a long history with eating disorders and negative body image.

'I knew that pregnancy would be a time where my body would go through significant changes that were entirely beyond my control, so I tried to be very mentally aware and prepared for the unknown. However, during both my pregnancies, I was extremely ill for the first 20 weeks,' she told me.

'I was vomiting multiple times a day, which brought up horrendously painful memories of my struggles with bulimia. I was also unable to eat anything but dry toast, so I was worried that I wasn't getting sufficient nutrients, which also brought up memories of my eating disorder days.

'As I continued further into my pregnancies, and my body began to grow, and change in ways I never expected, I found myself constantly trying to justify why these changes were taking place. I felt uncomfortable and awkward for the first six months even though I was so excited; it was a challenging and overwhelming time.'

Jess helped herself mentally with yoga throughout her pregnancies, so I asked her what tips she had for others: 'Firstly, it's important to know that what you are feeling and thinking is normal! Research shows that pregnancy is a significant time in a woman's life where negative body image issues can emerge, even if a woman has never experienced negative thoughts or feelings about her body before. But if you are concerned and you feel that you need some extra guidance, organisations such as The Butterfly Foundation have wonderful support for pregnant and postnatal women.'

Now it's time to work on the body shame! Who is with me?

Life is too short to beat ourselves up about back fat, flabby arms or a bulging belly. I know, I am incredibly lucky that I have been chosen by this precious soul to be his mum, and I need to show him what really matters in life. And it ain't what we look like.

IF I DIE TOMORROW, I SURE AS HELL DON'T WANT TO HAVE LIVED MY LAST DAY WORRIED ABOUT WHAT THE FUCK I LOOKED LIKE.

MY NEW INNER VOICE

After Memphis Ari Anderson Griffiths was born, my entire relationship with the way I saw myself changed. The shift started when I was 30 weeks pregnant. I still remember clear as day standing on the beach in Broome, Western Australia, in my newly purchased bikini, thinking, *I will not pass on this negativity to my unborn child, he or she will not speak to themselves the way I have.* It was from that day forward that I made the promise to love myself unconditionally like I would my child.

I was 35 years of age and 30 weeks pregnant when I decided to buy a bikini and wear it, and it changed my entire life. And if we are being super real, if this didn't happen, I am not sure if I would be writing this book.

One of my mates suggested I buy a bikini when I told her I was looking for swimmers for our babymoon. At first, I thought she was crazy and ignored her terrible idea. I've spent my entire life hiding my belly. But, while I was trying on swimmers in Target just before we left, I kept hearing her voice say, 'Who cares what people think? You're pregnant!' In that moment, I decided yep, fuck it, YOLO, this might be the only time I ever rock a two-piece and let it all hang out. So, I bought the $30 bikini, and I have rocked every part of me, while wearing it.

The day I put it on and strutted to the beach, Griffo was shocked. He honestly couldn't believe what he was seeing. I had him take at least 5000 photos of me in the bikini with my bump out because in my whole existence on earth I have only ever worn a bikini twice! And, on those couple of occasions, I was still giving a shit and caring what people thought.

The very first time I wore a bikini was for Instagram. I'd lost heaps of weight and just pretended my body image issues had gone with the weight loss, so I could get a pic, and write an inspirational message next to it.

Looking back, it was all so fake and just for validation. I still had so much hate towards my body and myself. The second time was in Cuba. Once again, I'd lost a heap of weight so thought, *Stuff it, I'll wear a bikini.* But after just one swim, I felt self-conscious and uncomfortable; I binned it and I went back to wearing a full-piece swimsuit.

The sense of freedom I felt on that beach in Broome that day hasn't left me.

Not caring about what I look like, not caring what people think, and not stopping to think about being pale or concerned about my cellulite, back flab or tummy rolls is an attitude I genuinely hope to pass on to my son.

It wasn't easy, but every day I made small changes to my mindset. Whenever I saw myself starting to talk negatively about my body, I changed the story. Every BODY has a story, and Every BODY deserves to be celebrated for all its glory. I no longer want to waste time hating on myself. I want to celebrate all my beautiful imperfections. So instead of calling myself a fat fuck, or a disgusting, ugly cow, I started to celebrate me and change to a new inner voice that had the following mantras:

Every BODY needs to be loved.
Every BODY has a story to tell.

I've always been petrified of dying: hello, anxiety! But having a child really made me think about my mortality more than ever before and, I know this sounds dark, I'd just birthed my baby boy, but this train of thought really changed my perspective on life.

Was I living my best life if I died tomorrow? Because tomorrow is not guaranteed for any of us, so have I given life my best shot today? I thought long and hard about this one. I had wasted years and years worrying about what people thought of me, how many calories I had eaten that day and how much exercise I had done. If I die tomorrow, I sure as hell don't want to have lived my last day worried about what the fuck I looked like. The time was now. I needed to fuck these hang-ups off in 2019 and show the world how amazing our bodies are and give myself the love and kindness I deserve.

So, days after my son was born, I stood in front of the mirror, pulled my pants down so I could see my C-section scar and I changed the story.

I cried, 'This is me and my beautiful tummy.'

For years I hid it from the world. I wouldn't even let Griffo touch it. As I looked at my tummy, I said to myself, 'I need to show my son how to love my body for all it does. Every BODY has rolls when they sit, so fuck it, today I'll let mine hang out.'

A quote I live by, which is not mine and from an unknown source is 'To lose confidence in one's body is to lose confidence in oneself. Take care of your body. It's the only place you have to live in. To love yourself as you are is a miracle, and to see yourself is to have found yourself, for now.'

After capturing myself at this moment with a picture of all my beautiful wobbly bits, I decided to sit down and write Memphis a letter, a promise to both of us from this day forward.

To my dearest son Memphis,

THANK YOU for teaching me to LOVE my body in all its glory.

For years, I hated on myself and battled loving all my wobbly bits, but something happened in pregnancy carrying you.

I made a promise to teach you and show you what true love was.

I promise to respect myself and honour my body and all it has endured.

My body made you. It created you, all of you.

Your little fingers and your little toes

And then it carried you for nine whole months, how clever is that?

Never again will I take my body for granted. Life is too short to waste years hating on it!

On September 5th it wasn't just you who was born ... I was too, your mum!

And I promise to never waste another second beating myself up because of what I've eaten or what I look like. My beautiful pouch will always be a reminder of you, Memphis Ari Anderson Griffiths.

My beautiful boy, I promise to guide you through life and show you, through my own behaviour how to love and embrace ourselves and that beauty is more than what you look like.

I love you.

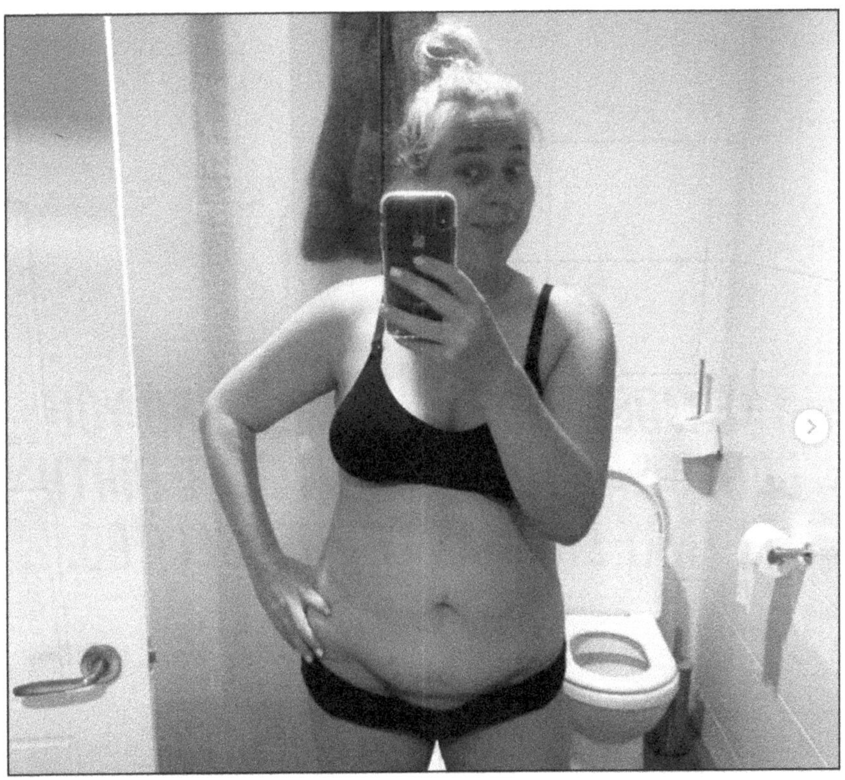

I posted this letter with my postpartum tummy pics on my socials and it was published by news outlets, talking about how brave I was to post such pics. I love that the media got around this conversation and had my toilet selfie go viral. We need to normalise women's bodies for all the shapes, sizes and overhangs they have, especially post-baby. But I don't believe it was brave to do so. This is WHY this conversation and chapter is important to have, because this should just be the norm.

"

THE MOST DETRIMENTAL THING YOU COULD SAY TO A WOMAN POST-BIRTH IS THAT SHE HAS LET HERSELF GO.

YOUR BODY, YOUR BUSINESS

I couldn't believe the focus on my body after I had Memphis. When I told people I had just had a baby the first thing they'd do is look at my tummy. I had loads of comments about my weight after giving birth and people glorifying how I've bounced back. The old me fed off compliments like this, but the new me knows how detrimental this can be to my mental health and to other mothers.

I'd be lying if I said my inner mean girls' ears didn't prick up when they heard compliments like this. Of course, they loved to hear things like, 'You look so skinny, Heidi, did you even have a baby?'

But I know better now.

This conversation is bigger than me, and I want to see women supported post-birth for their mental health and celebrated for what their bodies did, rather than play into the narrative that we need to bounce back quickly. The most detrimental thing you could say to a woman post-birth is that she has let herself go. Comparison Cassie would love this!

Why does it actually fucking matter what our bodies look like? Why does it matter to everyone else how much weight we've lost? Or how we look?

Our bodies have just created a life, then birthed a baby.

We have grown arms, legs, toenails, hearts, lungs and brains. We have just created little people of the future, but we are focusing on the body of the GODDESS who helped carry, grow and birth a miracle? This pressure really has to fucking stop.

Here are some words of wisdom for you to live by whenever you get caught in the vicious cycle:

> To all of you carrying beautiful pieces of art on your body, post-baby or not, let's celebrate. Remind yourself that if you are covered in those beautiful tiger stripes, they are yours to keep forever, and patterns are in.
>
> If you still have curves and excess weight, remember that it's more for your lover to hold on to! Rock your curves and embrace them. Tomorrow isn't guaranteed.
>
> If your pouch is still there months, weeks or years later, who gives a flying fuck?
>
> Next time you go to compliment a new mum on her post-baby body, stop and think about the amazing life she's 'grown', and whether it really matters what she looks like.
>
> Celebrate the goddess creating and birthing the miracle!

“

I WAS ADDICTED TO THAT CASH FLOW AND THE FAME OF THAT LIFE, BUT SOMETHING HAPPENED ON MY MATERNITY LEAVE ... I FOUND PEACE.

BORN TO BE A MUM

As I sit here typing away, Memphis has just woken up and I realise that I couldn't be further from the girl I once was.

I decided not to return to the radio airwaves in December 2019. I know, WTF!? I have become everything I once feared. My biggest concern was losing who I once was and that fear became a reality after Memphis was born, but I couldn't be more excited and pumped with who and where I am today. The thought of returning to work was giving me extreme anxiety. I realised when I was pushing Memphis along the beach on one of our early morning strolls that life was too short to go back to work for the pay packet. For so long I was addicted to the money, but I realised pretty soon after I had him that money is helpful and can buy nice things, but it's not everything. I had all I needed in my arms. I was addicted to that cash flow and the fame of that life, but something happened on my maternity leave … I found peace.

Stepping out of the radio bubble made me realise that my job was a huge trigger for me and for the first time in 10 years, I felt free from my inner demons. My entire identity was attached to that radio show so to not return in 2020 was a big bloody deal but by far the best thing I've ever done. I did wonder how I would survive outside the radio game if I was to ever leave. What would I do? Where would I work? Could I go back to a 9 to 5 job? But that fear kept me in a bubble that wasn't always the best for my mental health.

I wanted to quit on several occasions, but I was too scared. Scared of the unknown.

And here I am, almost three years into my post-radio life and I can tell you I have never felt so aligned with where I am today.

I was born to be Memphis' mum.

I was born to be free.

I was born to feel authentic.

And I was born to be me.

> **_YOU DON'T CHANGE IN THE COMFORT ZONE. STEPPING OUT OF IT IS WHAT MAKES YOU GROW._**

LIFE AFTER RADIO

After leaving radio, life took on a whole new meaning.

My mission was to share my truth with the world and support women on their journey of self-love and acceptance. My son, Memphis, had awakened a part of me that I was so desperate to find before him and I was ready to show the world who I was.

In January 2020, Shed Your Shit my movement and my new business venture, was born.

This movement has changed my life and thousands of others. It started off as a free swim and photo shoot in January 2020 with 30 strangers coming together to shed their shit in my very first workshop at the beach.

What happened that day was pure magic and it was the start of what has been an incredible couple of years. Thirty strangers came together, held each other's hands and cheered one another on, their mission to embrace themselves just as they are.

So many of us carry around baggage, whether it's past or current relationships, the relationship we have with ourselves, food, mental health, body demons … and in this moment like-minded women came together to strip off and share their vulnerabilities and let them go or as I like to say, 'SHED OUR SHIT'.

This moment signified a new beginning, not just for these legends but for me too.

My identity had, for a very long time, been associated with my job. As I trust in the process and the universe taking me into the next phase of my life, I want to say a massive THANK YOU to these amazing souls for sharing this moment with me.

You don't change in the comfort zone. Stepping out of it is what makes you grow.

I want to remind you also, that it doesn't take having a baby for you to have these breakthroughs. It is possible for you to make these changes and share in these moments and Shed Your Shit without the baby.

Thank you to all these gorgeous souls who rocked up to my very first FREE event to SHED THEIR SHIT. This chapter is for YOU!

"

IT KIND OF FELT LIKE I HAD FAILED, LIKE EVERYTHING I HAD DONE IN THE PAST DIDN'T MATTER ANYMORE AND I WASN'T GOOD ENOUGH.

GRIEVING FOR MY OLD LIFE

I want to be really honest here: although I have talked about the amazing transformation I have felt since leaving radio, it hasn't all been rainbows and butterflies.

I felt immense grief at times.

My entire identity was aligned with working in radio for just shy of 10 years. I thought this was the only job I would ever do and I wanted to get to Melbourne or Sydney breakfast radio. For years I craved this and dreamt about it every day. Just before I fell pregnant, one year prior to me leaving radio, I was auditioning for a Sydney breakfast show to be the female host with two others. I couldn't believe I was given the opportunity. I had so much fun in those auditions but something didn't feel aligned at the time. A week after my last audition, I received a call from one of my favourite mentors to say I had just missed out and the gal who got the job (who is a fucking legend btw and one of my dear radio sisters) had got the job. He said it was close and they were really impressed but it wasn't my time.

I was actually okay; I honestly felt like there was something else coming that was better.

And … there was.

His name is Memphis.

I loved being in a radio studio, most of the time ... I worked with some polar opposite personalities and at times I was crippled with self-doubt, angst, anxiety and intense imposter syndrome.

When I left, I had to grieve for the end of that chapter.

I had to grieve the friendships that I lost. I still remember my last on-air shift before I went on maternity leave: I cried like it was my last show ever; little did I know it would be.

I haven't really talked about this because it's hard to put into words, but I lost a massive chunk of myself when I left. The text messages and the likes on Instagram slowly started to stop, from people who I thought were my friends, until I had just a handful of mates left from the industry.

It made me question everything.

I remember announcing Memphis' birth live on the radio, the morning after he was born, and I felt empty. I really felt like I was stuck between two worlds. My son was in the neonatal ward after being taken from me only 30 minutes after getting to our room after an emergency C section. He had really low blood sugar and I couldn't move to the floor downstairs to hold him until the next morning.

I felt so much pressure to announce the arrival of my son to all of Perth because I had shared so much of my life in the past. And that's part of the job, it's what you do in radio, so I called in less than 24 hours after Memphis was born.

I wish someone had said to me, 'Get yourself sorted with your feeding, snuggle your little one with your hubby and when the time is right, we will announce it. We can keep it a secret until then.'

Had I known what an emotional roller-coaster motherhood would be, I would have done it differently.

But People-pleaser Polly thought I should phone into the show, because that's what good girls do.

In that moment I had never felt more alone and I had no idea who I was. I had a baby and I was now a mother but it didn't feel like it, because Memphis was in neonatal care and I hadn't even had a chance to properly meet him, or even be alone with him.

I felt like a stranger phoning into the show. It had only been three weeks since I left, but it felt like years. From that day, everything was different.

I had to remove myself from seeing anything about the radio show as it was triggering me and I felt more and more like an outsider.

I barely spoke to anyone from the building.

I was a new mum and my whole world had changed and I was worried about fitting in when I came back.

I reached out to friends in the industry. A friend from a sister station in Brisbane who is a beautiful human and radio soul sister, reassured me that everything was going to be okay and to get back to snuggling my new man. The feelings I was having were very real, but I should stay focused on my new baby.

Sleep deprivation was triggering my anxiety on the daily in the early days. I now understand why they say 'you are in the trenches.'

I struggled to let go and switch off. For so long, this radio show and studio was my baby, it was such a huge part of my life and now it felt like a distant memory.

My thoughts would run wild in the middle of the night or when Griffo was at work.

'Why hasn't anyone messaged me? They must want me off the show.'

'OMG look what they did on the show today; they look like they get along so well. What if they don't want me to come back?'

'What if I leave, what would I do? What would happen?'

'They must've never liked me in the first place.'

'Was I ever good at radio?'

These thoughts would get really loud, especially if I had little sleep and had been on social media.

It kind of felt like I had failed, like everything I had done in the past didn't matter anymore and I wasn't good enough.

A radio icon and someone who I look up to and absolutely love to death also reached out to me and told me to enjoy every single second and not waste another moment overthinking, all that mattered was in my arms.

This reminder was what I needed. I muted all my mates on the show on social media to stay sane.

It's funny how things work out, because what I feared the most – leaving radio – happened and it has been the best thing. Not only do I get to spend every single morning waking up with my little legend son, I have had so many incredible opportunities come my way because of the things I have created, not because I am the girl on the radio.

“

YOU NEED TO BE YOUR OWN BIGGEST CHEERLEADER AND BEST FRIEND.

CHANGING MY STORY

The change starts with you and no-one else. I want a world of women supporting women. I know you do too. I can't change the past but I can create the future and so can you.

I want a world where women love themselves and each other. A world of less hate, comparison and judgement!

Repeat after me ...

I am brave.

I am loved.

I am strong.

I am confident.

I am enough.

I am a miracle.

AND repeat daily!

Today is a miracle. You woke up. You're alive. I cannot hold your hand forever; the next step is up to you.

I can cheer fucking loudly for you and please know I am doing that right now.

You need to be your own biggest cheerleader and best friend.

Your power comes from within you and your own self-belief. No-one will cheer louder than you, for you! You should always be your number ONE fan.

I believe in you, now please go and start to show yourself the same love.

CHOOSING TO RADICALLY LOVE AND ACCEPT YOURSELF MEANS THAT AT TIMES YOU WILL RUB PEOPLE UP THE WRONG WAY.

UNAPOLOGETICALLY ME

Becoming unapologetically me has been a journey and a ride that sometimes I really wanted to get off. When you choose to put yourself out there like I have for the greater good, you can be crucified for everything about yourself, including your looks, personality, the way you write and the way you show up in the world, just as I have shared with you throughout this book.

It hasn't been easy to read the things people have said about me, or to be confronted by my past behaviour, but I know there is a bigger conversation around this. So, what I am unapologetic for is how I choose to show up today. By being unapologetically me. This doesn't mean I am not sorry for things that I have said, done or am, it means that I accept what I have done in the past and I forgive myself for it. I accept myself for who I am today.

Self-love is self-acceptance.

Choosing to radically love and accept yourself means that at times you will rub people up the wrong way. Some people may even see you as arrogant or just plain crazy, but that is their story, not yours.

By being unapologetically me, I have chosen to love myself warts and all.

I am far from perfect, and I do not claim to be. My hope is that by sharing my stories others will feel less alone.

We all have those inner critics in our heads, and mine still show up at times, and they always will. Hell, they are here now as I write this book!

These days they don't hang around as long because I am aware of them and I accept them. Fighting these voices has been a long road, as you have just read, and I hope you realise now that you too can get rid of the negative self-talk and be drunk on confidence too. I am not special or lucky, I just chose to do the work on understanding myself and becoming my own best friend.

Sunday nights these days are very different. I am normally in bed fast asleep by 8pm next to Griffo. I haven't felt the Anxiety Monster on my chest in years on a Sunday, because I chose differently, and you can too.

Falling in love with myself and building my confidence has been one of the best decisions I have ever made, and the only high I need these days. Becoming unapologetic about my body and accepting my imperfect self, by walking through shopping centres in my bra and undies, with my #walkofnoshame is how I do it. This is my process; this is being drunk on confidence.

This is more than just a book about me; it's a way to live your life and my hope is that you are OPEN to alternate practices and you take time out for you!

I know anxiety and fear can stop you from progressing and trying new things, but you need to tell yourself that you cannot grow, heal and build confidence unless you are open to stepping out of your comfort zone.

The definition of insanity is doing the same thing over and over and expecting a different result, and that is what I did for years. In the end, I truly felt like I was going insane.

I made the commitment to myself to be open and try new things for the sake of my own sanity and I am so glad I did that because I discovered things about myself that I never knew. Some things worked and others didn't, and this will be the same for you. All these experiences have led me to where I am today. Take whatever serves you from each experience; it could be life-changing or just start with one small thing. Remember 1 per cent daily changes = 365 per cent in one year.

It's taken me 10 years to get to where I am today, and I am still a work in progress.

Now it's your turn to be Drunk on Confidence.

Heidi x

You get ONE life, that's it!

This is how I live mine …

I don't care:

- If the random stranger on the beach thinks I'm fat in my bikini.
- If the random stranger on social media doesn't think I'm aesthetically pleasing or filtered enough.
- If the parents at the park think I'm a picture-perfect mum or not.

Stop giving away your power and stop giving a shit what people think!

ACKNOWLEDGEMENTS

Before we say, 'See you later', I have a final thought for you to ponder. If today was your last day, would you eat the cake? Would you wear the bikini? Would you care what the stranger thought of you on Instagram?

I know what I'd be fucking doing. I would eat the cake, while wearing the bikini, then post it on Instagram with all my belly rolls hanging out, saying, 'Fuck you' to the stranger on Insta who dares to judge me. Promise me that from this day forth, you will *stop* giving a fuck what people think of you.

We only have this moment.

Tomorrow isn't guaranteed.

So, if you take anything from this book, it's to live in the now because that's all we have. Thank you, Eckhart Tolle, for guiding me to the *now.* It took me a long time to get to this place and I couldn't have done it without the amazing spiritual leaders from around the world who I switched on daily through YouTube, social media and podcasts to guide me through some real shitstorms.

To my old boss Amanda Lee, thank you for encouraging me to share my story about anxiety publicly, you changed the trajectory of my life and I will be forever grateful. Also, to Will and Woody my radio co-hosts at the time, thank you for holding me in the studio that day and seeing me in my vulnerability.

I could sit here and write for days about the people who have helped me and guided me in some way, but my anxiety has me worried I'll forget someone. So, I'll say this …

Thank YOU to every single one of you, you know who you are. I couldn't have done it without you.

Thank YOU for believing in me, supporting, guiding and cheering me on! I fucking LOVE YA GUTS!

To my squad, and you the reader, YOU inspire me every day, keep rocking! We are in this together and you are not alone.

To my team at Big Sky Publishing – especially you, Sharon – thank you for choosing me and saying, 'Let's do this!' Your support, guidance, belief and trust has been incredible and I am forever grateful. It would not be possible without you. Biggest LOVE!

Massive love to my very first editor, Natasha Gilmour, who believed in me from our very first phone call and to my legendary friend Josh Langley, thank you! You know what you did! I love you and I'm eternally grateful.

To the amazing photographers who have captured the many moments of my life Chelsea Bates, Fliss & Co, Belle Verdiglione, Biz Coach and Photographer and Jillian McHugh Weddings. These photos are constant reminders of how far I've come. Thank you.

I want to acknowledge my parents, Kim and Steve; thank you for showing me that I could be anyone I want and achieve anything I want in life. Because of you, I have chased and accomplished more in 38 years than some people will in a lifetime. You are both incredible human beings and the best parents anyone could ever ask for.

To my first ever best friend, Nick, my brother, I wish you knew how much I admire and look up to you. I know times have been tough between us, but I love you, and you will always be my very first mate.

My soul sisters, you know who you are, thank you for all the crazy shenanigans, the late-night phone calls, the lols and for always accepting and seeing every part of me. I wouldn't be who I am today if it wasn't for you all.

Lastly, I want to thank my boys, Griffo, my hubby, and my son, Memphis. You two are by far the best thing to ever happen to me and I am forever grateful that you chose to do life with me. You are my biggest fans and I am yours. Thank you for all that you are; you have already taught me more than I can ever teach you. I love you both.

ABOUT THE AUTHOR

HEIDI ANDERSON ISN'T YOUR AVERAGE ANYTHING.

A perfectly imperfect combination of no BS and bang-on wisdom, she's the top-rating radio presenter and TV personality *turned* PR queen, Memphy's mum, Griffo's misso, self-love & mental health advocate, author and host of the chart-topping podcast, *Champagne Confidence*.

Heidi made headlines in 2012 and 2016 after announcing her struggle with chronic anxiety live on air. Her story went on to reach over 2 million people online. Since then, Heidi's shared her real and relatable journey from self-loathing to self-love and unwavering confidence with her community and is considered a leader in women's empowerment.

Never one to shy away from *taboo* topics, Heidi was born to be on stage where she speaks confidently and completely unfiltered. Her keynote gigs have been described as '*entertaining*', '*engaging*', '*inclusive*' and '*stand-out*'. A professional Hype Queen with a dream of taking her stage show on the road, she inspires women worldwide to love themselves as they are.

Single handedly disrupting the world of PR, Heidi launched her coaching programs in true Heidi style (flying a plane down WA's coast with a 'Heidi Anderson - the Queen of PR' banner and strutting through shopping centres in just a bra and undies, *obviously*). After 15 years in the media, she makes demanding attention look and feel effortless.

Madly typing this 'about the author' section in third person before her editor loses her shit, Heidi is currently sitting pantless (and *let's be honest*, probably braless) in Perth, Western Australia.

If you're keen on Shedding your Shit, Becoming Memorable AF, PRing the Shit out of Yourself, or miss my dulcet tones in your ears, scan the QR code below for links to my *Champagne Confidence* podcast and coaching programs.

www.heidileeanderson.com

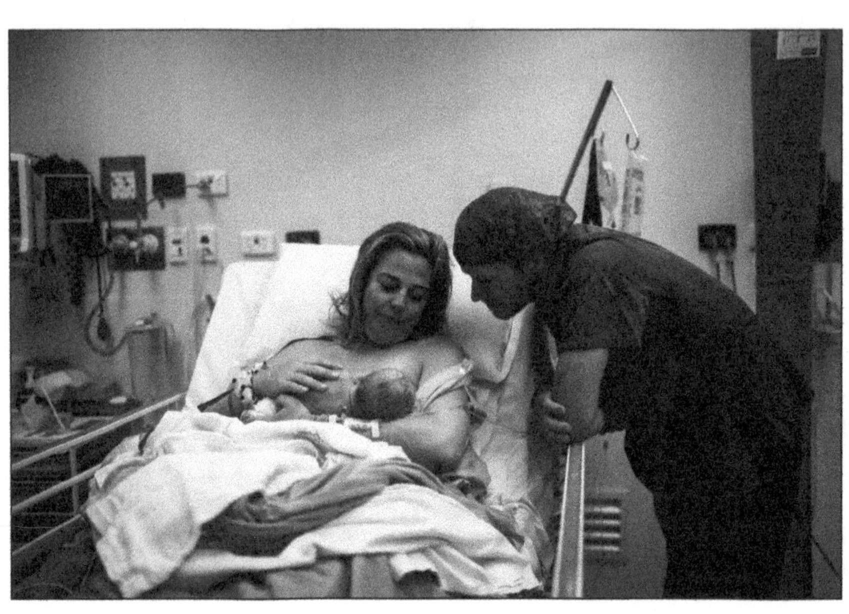

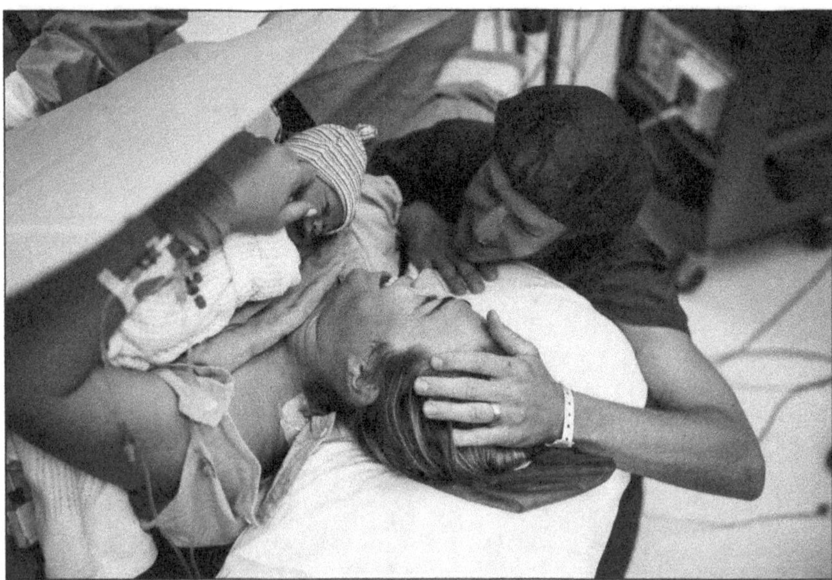